COSMETOLOGY CAREER STARTER

SCIENCE & TECHNOLOGY
14 DAYS

COSMETOLOGY
career starter

2nd edition

Lorraine Korman
with Felice Primeau Devine

LearningExpress

New York

Library of Congress Cataloging-in-Publication Data:
Korman, Lorraine
   Cosmetology career starter / Lorraine Korman, with Felice Primeau Devine—2nd ed.
     p. cm
   Includes index.
   ISBN 1-57685-397-7 (pbk.)
   1. Beauty culture—Vocational guidance—United States. I. Devine, Felice Primeau. II.
   Title
   TT958 .K67 2002
   646.7'2'02373—dc21

                                        2001038995

Printed in the United States of America
9 8 7 6 5 4 3 2 1
Second Edition

ISBN 1-57685-397-7

For more information or to place an order, contact LearningExpress at:
   900 Broadway
   Suite 604
   New York, NY 10003

Or visit us at:
   www.learnatest.com

Contents

Contents

Introduction

Why Enter the Beauty Services Profession?

FOR STARTERS, the beauty services industry is practically impervious to downturns in the economy. In fact, job demand in the beauty industry is projected to remain strong through the foreseeable future. Recent surveys and studies of the industry report that demand for beauty professionals outweighs qualified applicants.

In addition to being a growth industry, cosmetology is also one of the most creative, flexible, and diverse career paths. Cosmetologists can express their creativity as hairdressers, skincare specialists, nail technicians, massage therapists, makeup artists, or all of the above. The possibilities in the beauty field are as many and varied as the individuals in the field. It's truly an occupation in which you can create your own path.

As you decide to create that path, it is important to recognize that there are a few key traits that successful cosmetologists share. Typically they:

▶ Enjoy dealing with the public
▶ Can take direction from clients
▶ Can tolerate long hours spent standing
▶ Are good with their hands
▶ Have a pleasant demeanor and are willing to put aside a bad mood when at work
▶ Are committed to staying on top of and learning the latest techniques
▶ Have an interest in fashion and beauty trends

You will learn more about what it takes to succeed as a cosmetologist in Chapter 6.

JUST THE FACTS

The *1999 Job Demand Survey of the Cosmetology Industry*, conducted by the National Accrediting Commission of Cosmetology Arts and Sciences, reports that "the salon industry continues to be a job-seekers market. This is especially exciting news for recent graduates and individuals wanting to re-enter the field."

When people think about beauty services professionals, they often picture people working in a salon. But just as hairdressing is only one of many areas of specialization, working in a salon is only one of many places where beauty professionals can build their careers. They can find work on television and movie sets, in theaters, at department stores, in the fast-paced world of magazine publishing, or as cosmetology instructors. Your specialty, personality, and where you live will help determine where you decide to develop your career. In this book you will learn more details about the possible paths you can take you can take as a beauty professional. In Chapter 1, you will learn more about the hottest careers for beauty professionals, what to expect from each, and whether or not they are right for you.

This book also covers training programs on the high school, vocational school, and postsecondary levels. You will learn what's required to get your license, and why getting your license is only the beginning of your career.

Interviews with top beauty professionals in every specialty appear throughout the book, providing you with valuable advice on what it takes to make it in the real world of cosmetology. These professionals share their own experiences and discuss changes in the beauty field. The appendices at the back of the book not only list the most important organizations in the field but also point you toward helpful resources (books, websites, and so on). Each of these resources has been completely updated for the second edition of this book.

To get the most out of this book, take a moment to look at what you will find in each chapter:

Chapter One	**Description**
The Hottest Careers for Beauty Professionals	This chapter will help you decide if a career as a beauty professional is a good choice for you. It describes the most popular and in-demand beauty services jobs, and provides an overview of typical job

responsibilities. It also contains salary surveys and other industry statistics.

Chapter Two

All About Cosmetology
Education Programs

This chapter will help you decide which type of training program is most appropriate for your needs and plans. It describes a variety of training programs, from high school to vocational school to post-secondary education, and provides sample course descriptions.

Chapter Three

Financial Aid for the Training
You Need

Once you have decided what type of training is for you, this chapter will provide you with more information about schools that offer cosmetology programs. This chapter also provides you with all the information you need to know about securing financial aid for the training program of your choice.

Chapter Four

How to Land Your First Job

This chapter explains how to find a job after you complete your training. It will lead you through the process of conducting your job search from networking to research, industry publications, classified ads, online resources, visiting job fairs, and contacting job hotlines.

Chapter Five

Resumes, Cover Letters,
and Interviews

This chapter will teach you how to create an effective cover letter and resume. It tells you the most important items to include—and to avoid—in your cover letter and resume. It also shows you what prospective employers look for during interviews.

Chapter Six

How to Succeed on the Job

In this chapter, you will discover valuable secrets for becoming the successful beauty professional you know you can be. You will learn about managing important work relationships, how to stay on top of new techniques, how to manage your time, and tips for developing a dedicated clientele.

Appendix A	This is a list of organizations dedicated to
Professional Associations	developing, educating, and supporting
and State Cosmetology Boards	beauty professionals. The list is arranged
	by specialty. Also, there is a complete list
	of State Boards on Cosmetology.
Appendix B	This is a list of helpful books, magazines,
Additional Resources	and websites that you can use as a refer-
	ence throughout your career.
Appendix C	
Sample Free Application for	
Federal Student Aid (FAFSA)	

By using this book, you will find out if a career in the beauty service industry is for you. Once you've done that, you will be on your way to becoming a successful cosmetologist. Let's start by discovering the hottest careers open to beauty service professionals.

CHAPTER one

THE HOTTEST CAREERS FOR BEAUTY PROFESSIONALS

THIS CHAPTER defines the term *cosmetologist* and the many different specialties in the professional beauty field. It will highlight the hottest careers for cosmetologists, explaining the tasks that people who specialize in these areas typically perform. You will see examples of job descriptions and sample salaries, and discover what current cosmetologists think about the profession. Most importantly, you will answer questions that will help you to decide whether or not a career in cosmetology is really for you.

EVEN IF you are just beginning to become interested in a career as a beauty professional, then you probably know that the beauty industry is booming. It seems that every day a new spa or salon is opening in towns and cities across the United States. Each season, beauty and fashion magazines tout new hairstyles, updated makeup styles, new skin-care techniques—all of which women (and men) who are concerned with their appearance cannot live without. And, thanks to the popularity of magazines like *In Style* and *People*, the beauty whims of Hollywood stars are detailed regularly and insider tips are common. Top hairdressers, colorists, makeup artists, and salon owners have risen to celebrity status themselves. Evidence that the beauty industry is experiencing success is everywhere.

Since they are such a part of everyday life—and they probably have played a large part in your life already—it is often easy to imagine what a cosmetologist's life is like. Maybe you picture your manicurist and think you'd enjoy a job where you use your hands, and the end result is beautiful hands for your clients. Or, maybe you picture beauty mogul Marcia Kilgore, founder of Bliss spas and products, and think that you have the creativity and know-how to develop new skin care techniques and treatments. Or, maybe you imagine Hollywood versions of cosmetologists' lives—from Craig Ferguson as the flamboyant Glasgow hairdresser in *The Big Tease* to the less-than-flattering "Beauty School Dropout" musical number from the movie *Grease*.

Whatever your mental picture—no one image can be entirely accurate. Successful beauty professionals today work in all sorts of capacities, with all sorts of specialties. Cosmetology is no longer just a field for people who feel that they can't do anything else, like Frenchy in *Grease* felt. Nor is cosmetology just a field for people with dreams of becoming as much a celebrity as their clients, like makeup artist and Stila founder, Janine Lobell. What cosmetology is, however, is both of those extremes and everything in between. Tens of thousands of success stories from across the country prove that cosmetology is a field with options, flexibility, and the potential to make a lucrative living. And, according to the *U.S. Occupational Outlook Handbook*, cosmetology is an industry that is expected to grow faster than average until at least 2008. What more could you ask for?

DEFINITION OF COSMETOLOGIST

While the dictionary definition of cosmetologist is "an expert in the use of cosmetics," the real-life definition is really so much more than that. From hairdresser to massage therapist to manicurist, a cosmetologist is a beauty professional who is licensed to perform services for the public. This table will give you an overview of the jobs that fall under the term cosmetologist:

Role	Description of Tasks
Hairdresser/Hair Stylist	Cuts, colors, perms, straightens, shampoos, conditions, and styles a client's hair. Haircoloring is a hot growth area for hairdressers, perms on the other hand have been decreasing in popularity over the past few years.

Nail Technician	Performs manicures and pedicures—cleaning and buffing nails, trimming or pushing back cuticles, painting with nail polish. Some nail techs apply extravagant nail art—air brushed images and jewels—to their clients' manicures or pedicures.
Electrologist	Performs electrolysis—permanent hair removal using an electrical current. This service can be performed at a salon or in a medical environment.
Esthetician	Provides a wide range of skin care services including hair removal, waxing, facials, and procedures designed to combat the effects of aging.
Makeup Artist	Applies makeup that is either temporary (cosmetics) or permanent (such as tattooed eyeliner). Makeup artists who work with cosmetics may do so in one or many of a variety of environments—salons, house calls, department stores, or theater.
Massage Therapist	Some of the types of massage a therapist may practice include Swedish, shiatsu, sports, reflexology, lymphatic drainage, Reiki, aromatherapy, rehabilitative, craniosacral, or polarity. Massage therapists can work in salons, spas, health clubs, cruise ships, hospitals, or private practice.
School Instructor	Develops objectives for a classroom, makes lesson plans, gives presentations, develops test questions, and, most important, helps students become successful beauty professionals.
Salon Manager	Coordinates all of the day-to-day activities and events that keep the salon running smoothly.

In some states, the cosmetology license permits you to perform nailcare, skincare, and makeup services as well as hairdressing. In other states, separate licensing procedures have been established for nail technicians and for estheticians. Electrologists, massage therapists, and permanent makeup artists almost always have to have separate licenses. To find out about certification in your state, go to Appendix A and contact your state board.

IS COSMETOLOGY FOR YOU?

Please respond *yes* or *no* to the following questions:

1. I consider myself a highly creative individual.
2. I thrive on structure; I like to know exactly what the next day will bring.
3. I'm good with my hands.
4. Given a choice, I'd work alone.
5. I wouldn't mind putting in extra hours to learn more about specialties in my field. I consider that an investment in myself.
6. More than anything, I want to work less than 40 hours a week but still make a good income.
7. I really enjoy working with people.
8. I just want a job that I don't have to think about when I'm off the clock.
9. I've been told that I have a way with people.
10. I'm pretty impatient. I get antsy easily.

If you answered *yes* to questions 1, 3, 5, 7, and 9, then you're probably a pretty good candidate for a cosmetology career. If, however, you answered *yes* to questions 2, 4, 6, 8, and 10, then you more than likely will not find a fulfilling career in cosmetology.

Why? Because cosmetology is, first and foremost, a service industry. Yes, it provides tremendous outlets for your creativity, but the success of beauty professionals—from the hottest editorial hairstylist to the first-year trainee—depends on your ability to service your client well, thoroughly, and with a smile. To do that, you need to be flexible—to be willing to rearrange your schedule to accommodate a last-minute client, for example. You also need to enjoy being around people all the time. Their happiness has to mean something to you. Few solitary types have ever thrived in a salon environment. If you think that you can thrive in a career in cosmetology, read on—it's time to learn a few quick facts about the industry.

INDUSTRY FACTS

In 1999, there were 297,000 salons in the United States and 1,286,000 licensed cosmetologists (according to a 2000 National Accrediting Commission of Cosmetology Arts and Sciences [NACCAS] report)—more than either the number of elementary school teachers or lawyers. You should note, however, that this figure includes a fair number of people who are licensed but not currently practicing. In fact, some estimates maintain that 20% of people who pass the state boards never even use their license.

The U.S. Bureau of Labor Statistics has projected that the number of jobs within the cosmetology industry will increase by approximately 10% between 1998 and 2008.

Salon cosmetologists are generally divided into three categories: full-time employees, part-time employees, and booth renters. The last are those who operate as independent contractors and pay a percentage of their gross income or a flat fee to the salon owner for the space they rent within a salon.

According to the NACCAS, almost 25% of the salon workforce consists of cosmetologists with less than 18 months of experience—a pretty good indication that there's entry-level work out there. Also, most new graduates start their careers working part-time in a salon, often as part of a salon-designed apprenticeship or training program.

According to NACCAS, the average income, including tips, for the average full-time salon professional is about $18.50 an hour or $38,000 a year. *Money* magazine ranked cosmetology the 37th of its "Fifty Hottest Jobs" according to its projected growth through 2005.

According to the Carousel Beauty Colleges Industry Outlook Report, women make up nearly 73% of the profession. In addition, over 89% of cosmetologists are white, 7.5% black, and 6.4% Hispanic. And, the majority of cosmetologists are between 30 and 45 years old.

To practice cosmetology, you must first attend a trade or a vocational school and receive a certain number of hours of training, then pass a state board exam in order to be licensed. The average fee for attending a postsecondary cosmetology school (curriculum usually takes 9–14 months to complete) is between $2,000 and $7,000. Specialized schools take even less time. Vocational or technical cosmetology programs at the high school level are administered by the public school system and most are free of charge. Some states require students to complete their education at the postsecondary level, however.

Job Market Controversy

There's substantial disagreement over the true state of the labor market in the salon industry. NACCAS reported in their Job Demand Survey that during 1999, salon owners had over 500,000 positions to fill; 75% of those also said that they had difficulty filling the positions with qualified applicants.

A report from the Cosmetology Advancement Foundation (CAF) estimates the stylist shortage by taking an annual industry growth rate of 2.14%—a conservative figure—and factoring in the number enrolled in beauty schools, the number who graduate, and the number of licensed stylists who leave the industry yearly. According to this formula, the project shortage for 1997 was 206,500. By the year 2000, the industry will have 345,000 unfilled jobs.

So, there's a labor shortage, right?

In 1997, the General Accounting Office (GAO) of the federal government issued a controversial report entitled "Proprietary Schools: Millions Spent to Train Students for Oversupplied Occupations." According to the report, there are almost five licensed cosmetology professionals for every current job opening—a *surplus* of trained workers; therefore, the report concludes, the government should not continue to fund training for cosmetology and other vocational occupations.

What does this mean to you? Well, since some 80% of students receive some sort of financial aid to attend beauty school, the answer is: plenty. Fortunately, industry associations, such as the International Chain Salon Association (ICSA), have been lobbying Washington for a new report. Their reasoning? ICSA alone claims to have 22,700 job openings among its members. Beauty industry insiders believe that because the GAO report never took into account whether licenses were active or inactive, its numbers are unrealistic. Additionally, some 80% of cosmetologists are women, many of whom leave the profession for personal reasons, such as to care for their children. And the GAO report made its claims based on statistics from state employment offices—and no salon owner turns to a state agency to fill a job vacancy. By the time this book went to press, the GAO had quietly rescinded its report, but reliable statistics remain an industry question mark.

Sample Job Description #1
Nail Technician/Manicurist

Fashion Time Event Management develops and manages event-marketing programs. Our Manicurists and Nail Technicians are independent contractors who work at promotional events such as the Great Bridal Expo, Day SPA USA, and many more health and beauty promotional events in other local markets.

Job Qualifications

- Trained and licensed as a manicurist
- Experienced in promoting professional and non-professional products (retail experience a plus)
- Excellent communication skills
- Energetic and outgoing
- 1–2 years professional manicurist experience

HOT JOBS AND CAREERS

Although there are limited types of licenses available for beauty professionals, the potential to break out of the box is enormous. "There are so many options in this industry. It's impossible to get bored being a beauty professional," says D.J. Freed, who owns Key Lime Pie Salon & Spa in Atlanta, Georgia. She should know. She began her career as a makeup artist in New York, then moved to Atlanta and began learning about hair, studying under the city's best hairdressers and eventually opened up her own business—all while doing photo shoot work with the likes of the Indigo Girls. It's an industry with a tremendous amount of room to move and grow. The following are just some of the career options available to beauty professionals.

Hairdresser

Hairdressers cut, color, perm, relax, shampoo, condition, and style a client's hair. They are the lifeblood of any full-service salon. The hairdresser's role has changed radically in the last 40 years, ever since Vidal Sassoon revolutionized the beauty industry with his radical geometric cuts. It may be hard to believe now, but before Sassoon, women of all ages visited the beauty salon weekly for their wash-and-sets. They often slept in their rollers (and this was before sponge rollers!) and didn't have the benefit of the more sophisticated products we have today. Sassoon changed the landscape of hairdressing forever. Since the early 1960s, the emphasis has been on the cut—preferably a low-maintenance but fashionable one.

Over the last ten years, hairdressing specialties have sprung up. Cosmetology used to mean that you did it all—cuts, chemical services, styling, and finishing. Maybe you even did your client's nails and gave her a facial too. While that's still true at many salons—and the more adept you are at a variety of services, the more marketable you will be—other salons have encouraged their staff members to specialize in one aspect of cosmetology. There are enough educational resources out there for anyone with the interest and talent to become a specialist in haircoloring, permanent waving, or chemical relaxing (also known as straightening).

It's important to think seriously about this because haircolor in particular has become a huge revenue stream for salons. Recent surveys have shown that up to 60% of American women color their hair, and many of them have it done in salons. There are a variety of reasons for this, including the aging baby-boomer population and the development of temporary demipermanent and semipermanent haircolors that require less commitment from the client. (It helps that they are also cheaper.) On the flip side, permanent waves have been decreasing for years, while relaxer services have increased dramatically. But because many women are frightened of botching their hair with a home-perm kit or a home-straightening kit, there will always be a market for salon chemical services. A bonus: They are high-ticket items that boost your personal bottom line.

Compensation and Prerequisites

All hairdressers need to be licensed to practice on a client. After licensing, you can go to work as an employee of a salon or as an independent contractor in a salon (also known as a booth renter), or you can even work at home. If you're an employee, you will be paid a straight salary, salary plus commission, or commission only. If you feel that entrepreneurial spirit coming on, you can start your own salon, although it's usually best to spend a few years learning the ropes before you jump into owning a business.

Specialization is usually the result of trying out different positions in a salon and finding the right fit. When you specialize, you are expected not only to exhibit unusual skill at the position—say, coloring—but also to stay on top of the trends by attending continuing education classes regularly, attending trade shows, and taking part in salon trainings. You might even want to offer a special model night at the salon in which you offer services to clients who are willing to let you experiment in exchange for a price break. It's a great way to stay creatively fresh *and* build your client base.

Did You Know?

The first hair dryers came on the market in the 1920s, but they were virtually unusable due to their bulk and propensity to overheat. It wasn't until the early 1950s that truly useable hair dryers made their way into beauty salons.

Source: About.com

Nail Technician

Nail techs, as they are sometimes called, are licensed to perform manicures and pedicures. They clean and buff nails, trim or push back cuticles, and paint nails with polish. As the popularity of nail art (such as elaborate designs and jewelry) has increased, nail techs have had to further hone their artistic skills. A good nail tech has a steady hand, a relaxed manner, and impressive powers of concentration. Nail techs can work in a variety of environments, including full-service salons, nails-only salons (increasingly popular), and spas, as well as on photo shoots. In many states, a separate nail tech test and license are offered.

Nails are a rapidly growing area of the salon industry; more and more women (and men) view them as part of a total fashion look. Roxana Pintile, co-owner of New York's Warren-Tricomi Salon and a nail technician for 16 years, says, "Not having your nails taken care of is like wearing a Chanel suit but having a run in your stocking." Clients have educated themselves, mostly through magazines, about nail health and the importance of taking care of their nails. And due to the ever-increasing number of women in the workforce, many of whom have to spend long days on their feet, pedicures are hugely popular, particularly when they incorporate massage.

To succeed as a nail technician, you need a sound aesthetic sense and an accommodating personality. "Talking to people and being a good listener are keys to doing well," says Pintile. "Read the newspaper every day so you can keep informed and have something to talk about. And study, study, study. Nails are constantly evolving. Listen to the client, too; give her what she wants. If she trusts you, she'll come out of her safety zone and start letting you suggest things to her."

Compensation and Prerequisites

As noted earlier, beauty professionals are paid either straight salary, salary plus commission, or strictly commission. In some cases—and this is particularly common for nail techs—the beauty pro simply rents space in a salon establishment and pays a flat monthly rate for the space. Anything above and beyond that, she keeps as income. This makes the nail tech an independent operator, not an employee.

Some salon owners look for nail techs with a client base, but experience is not usually their primary concern. It's whether you can give a great manicure. When looking for a position, offer to give the salon owner a manicure or pedicure. Your work will speak for itself.

Hot Job! Manicurist

Manicurists, or nail techs, are in high demand. Here is a sample of median salaries from various cities across the United States. Keep in mind that these salaries are *exclusive* of tips and commission. Some sources estimate that hot nail techs get up to 50% in tips—raising the income potential *dramatically.*

Albany, NY: $15,832

Indianapolis, IN: $15,191

Memphis, TN: $15,115

Baltimore, MD: $15,410

Columbus, OH: $15,199

Source: salary.com

Esthetician

It's a great time to be an esthetician. Esthetics, or skincare, is experiencing a boom of sorts, largely because baby boomers refuse to age. They're searching desperately for the product or service that will help them look and feel young. That's good news for skincare pros, who perform a variety of therapeutic skincare services, such as facials and waxing.

More and more full-service salons offer a full complement of skincare services. It's a way of marketing the salon as a resource for one-stop beauty shopping. Licensing generally takes under a year, and you can also work as an independent contractor. Many estheticians can also provide makeup services, hair removal and waxing, and body care services. Estheticians also work at day spas, in skincare-only facilities, and with dermatologists or plastic surgeons.

Are you surprised by the medical connection? Up until a few years ago, doctors generally dismissed the idea of facials. Now, treatments such as chemical peels, micro-dermabrasion, and scar-tissue therapy are often handled in a dermatologists office by an esthetician. Working with doctors may appeal to you if you're interested in treating traumatized skin, working in a clinical environment, or helping to heal post-operative patients.

If you're interested in esthetics, ask yourself the following questions:

▶ Am I a giving person? An esthetician needs to be concerned about other people, because he or she is a caregiver and wellness provider, as well as a facialist.
▶ Do I enjoy working closely with people?
▶ Can I handle seeing and touching damaged skin?
▶ Can I sit in one room all day? Or do I need to be out and about, walking around?

Making It

According to Barbara Salomone, president of the Conservatory of Esthetics postgraduate skincare facilities, with locations across America, there are ten requirements for a successful esthetician:

- the ability to work with people
- empathy
- patience
- sales know-how
- determination to succeed
- willingness to learn about new treatments and ideas
- the ability to market your positives
- willingness to work long hours and accommodate clients
- keeping in tune with skincare trends and the salon/medical environment
- the confidence to stand behind what you are doing

Compensation and Prerequisites

Most facilities require a license and experience, which you can often get working on the floor of your training facility. Again, use your beauty school's network as a referral system, and offer to assist someone for little or no charge as you learn the ropes. Compensation is similar to that of nail technicians.

Makeup Artist

Makeup artists often provide the finishing touches to a client. Their services are offered either as stand-alones or as value-added for salon clients after their hair is done. Makeup artists are often called upon to service clients at home or to work with groups or on special occasions, such as bridal parties. They can also work in department stores, in theater, television, or film.

Permanent makeup is a more labor-intensive service that can involve disguising a disfigurement, working with burn victims, or altering a client's pigmentation by, for instance, tattooing with a permanent eyeliner or lip liner. Permanent makeup artists usually work in a salon environment or on their own.

Compensation and Prerequisites

Most facilities require a license and experience, which you can often get working on the floor of your training facility. Again, use your beauty school's network as a referral system, and offer to assist someone for little or no charge as you learn the ropes. Compensation is similar to that of nail technicians.

Sample Job Description #2
Hair Stylist

A small, cozy salon needs hairstylists for a newly renovated salon. The right candidate should be an organized, motivated, and outgoing person with a positive, high-energy attitude and very professional presence. Good sales background with the ability to close sales with existing client base as well as new prospects is helpful. We offer training and base pay including commissions, plus a complete benefits package.

Duties include:

- Styling hair by cutting, shaping, combing, permanent waving, relaxing, coloring, and conditioning
- Explaining, promoting, and selling retail merchandise
- Maintaining customer records, especially hair coloring records
- Keeping work area clean, orderly, and safe; maintaining equipment and following prescribed safety measures

Requirements

- Current cosmetologist license
- Knowledge of cutting, shaping, permanent waving, relaxing, coloring, combing, and performing hair styling services and selling retail products
- Familiarity with hair and scalp treatments
- 1–2 years experience styling hair

Electrologists

Electrolysis is permanent hair removal using an electrical current. (The current reacts with salt in the body, creating sodium hydroxide, or lye, which damages the follicle so it will not produce hair.) Many states issue a separate license to electrologists rather than issuing them a general cosmetologist license. Electrologists can work in either a salon environment or a medical one. A growing number of spas offer electrolysis as well. Attention to detail, a soft touch, and an understanding of physiology are crucial components of this job. Perhaps more than any other beauty professionals, electrologists need to be sensitive as clients come to you with a variety of problems, each of which is very important to them. They appreciate discretion and understanding.

Compensation and Prerequisites

Most facilities require a license and experience, which you can often get working on the floor of your training facility. Again, use your beauty school's network as a referral system, and offer to assist someone for little or no charge as you learn the ropes. Compensation is similar to that of estheticians.

Keys to Success in a Salon

A willingness to learn. A great many beauty professionals say their education really began after school.

Talent. If you don't have dexterity, a creative eye, and a gentle, nurturing touch, cosmetology will prove a frustrating field.

The ability to juggle many tasks at once. In the beginning, you will probably be assisting a senior-level stylist and will be called upon to mix a color formula while shampooing another client and getting bobby pins for someone else. You will have to adjust to a fast-paced environment, because once you graduate to a higher position, you will often be working on multiple clients simultaneously.

Communication. Watch successful beauty professionals and you will notice that they are uniformly excellent listeners. They coax, cajole, and soothe the client in their chair. One well-known hairdresser calls his job "one-third artist, two-thirds psychotherapist." He's telling the truth.

Sample Job Description #3
Esthetician

Gina's Day Spa is looking for individuals with enthusiasm, team spirit, and the ability to work in a fast-paced environment who want to succeed in the fast-growing beauty industry. Candidates must have an up-to-date cosmetology license and a minimum of two years experience working as an esthetician.

Responsibilities include:

- Provide quality facial treatments
- Perform waxing treatments
- Educate clients on proper skincare regimens
- Create long-term relationships with clients
- Have a flexible schedule
- Promote and sell products
- Stay up-to-date on current market fashions and trends

Salon Owner

After a few years in the business, the entrepreneurial spirit kicks in among a high percentage of beauty professionals. Often, stylists and other specialists decide to strike out on their own and start their own business. It's not as easy as it sounds, though. Here are a few tips to help you find out whether ownership is the way to go:

Take some business courses at your local community college. They don't teach Accounting 101 in beauty school, but you will need to know it to run any business. Better to learn it in a classroom than the hard way.

Watch how things work in your salon. What's good about working there? What can be improved? What aspects of the operation don't you understand? Take notes on your impressions. Try to spend time helping out with as wide a variety of tasks as possible.

Join the National Cosmetology Association. It's a tremendous business resource.

Offer to help the owner with administrative or bookkeeping tasks. It will lend some perspective on the big picture.

Network with other salon owners. Ask them about the biggest challenges they face running a business. Their insights can give you a head start on tackling your own problems if you decide to run your own show.

Compensation and Prerequisites

Generally, business owners don't get a salary. You are paid out of the business's profits—which is great if your salon has a good year and disastrous if it has a bad one. Also keep in mind that before you can pay yourself, you have to pay overhead—staff salaries, rent, utilities, and any outstanding loans. That said, if you can get the appropriate financing, you can open a salon.

Sample Job Description #4
Massage Therapist

Muscle Mania Gym is seeking qualified massage therapists for both full- and part-time positions at various locations within our organization. Candidates should be able to perform various techniques in the art of massage therapy. Therapists will also have the opportunity to increase their client base and earn more by providing personal training services at our gyms. Therapists who are not currently qualified to train can gain certification through our paid, in-house training programs. Muscle Mania also offers a competitive base salary, commissions, 401(k), and benefits (medical and dental) for full-time employees.

Required Skills:

- Massage Therapy license
- Personal insurance (i.e., AMTA, IMA, etc.)
- Current CPR certification
- Exceptional organizational skills
- Excellent verbal and written communication skills
- Outstanding customer service skills

Salon Manager

Some professionals enjoy running the show—coordinating everything having to do with the day-to-day running of a salon operation. Good salon managers are worth their weight in gold. They handle issues such as who gets the walk-in clients, what the special promotion of the month will be, and when the toilet will get fixed. They also are in charge of hiring staff and conflict resolution. They play an important role because many salon owners have the entrepreneurial spirit but lack management know-how. Those who realize this know the value of a good salon manager. For more information, refer to *Milady's Successful Salon Management for Cosmetology Students* by Edward J. Tezak (Delmar, 2001).

Compensation and Prerequisites

A salon manager at a medium-to-large establishment (they are seldom needed at small salons) is usually paid a weekly salary without commission or tips. These salaries can run from $25,000 up to $80,000 per year for the highest level positions.

To fill a management role, salon owners look for someone who is extremely organized, mature, and detail-oriented. You will have to demonstrate understanding of an accounting spreadsheet as well as the fragile human ego. For these reasons, someone with managerial experience is usually ideal. However, a growing number of beauty schools offer a salon-management track to formally prepare those who love the salon environment, but don't want to spend their time behind a chair.

If you are a recent grad who didn't get the opportunity to get some formal training but think management might be the thing for you, then shadow your own salon manager. Ask to assist him or her. You will learn plenty about the demands of the job and what it takes.

What Do Students Like about a Cosmetology Career?

Meeting new and interesting people

Good income

Flexible hours and location

The opportunity to become your own boss

Job availability, high employment rate

Fun, interesting work

Source: Procter & Gamble 1995 national survey,
"Who Are the Cosmetology Students of Tomorrow?"

Hairdresser or Makeup Artist for Film, TV, or Theater

Sachiko Yanase has been involved in editorial hair styling for 15 years. In addition to magazine photo shoots, she has worked on numerous commercials, TV sets, movies, and fashion shows.

A native of Osaka, Japan, her first job was as a stylist for a TV show in Tokyo. She was lucky to have a good friend and client who worked in the industry; when her friend needed someone to hire a stylist for a new show, she called Sachiko. The well-placed connection helped her to get involved in the fast-paced, exciting world of editorial hair styling.

Eight years ago, Sachiko moved to the United States and found a job working in a beauty salon in New York. She was eager to get involved in freelance work but she had no contacts in the industry here. She didn't know anyone working in TV or on movies. She didn't know any photographers. So, she went out and pounded the pavement and made a name for herself as a top-rate freelance stylist.

Sachiko found photographers who were looking for stylists to help with test shoots. These were excellent opportunities for her because while they did not pay, they gave her a chance to highlight her skills and build her portfolio. For two years, she spent almost every weekend on test shoots. At night, she went to every party that she heard about—in case there would be photographers to whom she could introduce herself. Her day and night approach paid off. She is now known in the industry and is able to pick and choose her assignments.

Since Sachiko is neither in a union or represented by an agency, she is responsible for getting her jobs. Most of them come from photographers who have worked with her in the past. Once they find out that she is skilled, reliable, and creative, they recommend her to their friends, clients, and colleagues.

A benefit to working on photo shoots, fashion shows, and movies is that Sachiko is able to easily stay on top of every trend. This enables her to provide her clients at the beauty salon with advice that keeps them fashionable and up-to-date. She loves the freedom of freelance work but more than that she loves meeting new people and learning new skills from them. She also enjoys being able to express her creativity while working on photo shoots and fashion shows. Some of the wildest styles she's ever created have been for fashion shows.

There is no typical freelance job. Sachiko says that some jobs pay her by the day, some by the hour, and some by the project. For some jobs, she is told exactly what to do. For others, she has free reign to create the style she wants. Similarly, for low-budget films, she often does make-up as well as hair styling while for most shoots, commercials, and shows she is limited to styling hair.

Freelance editorial hair styling is a fascinating world, and it is a part of her career that she would never give up. What advice does she have for cosmetologists who want to get involved in editorial work? "Meet new people." Networking is key. Getting you name and portfolio out there, making connections, and staying on top of trends are important to becoming a successful editorial stylist.

Compensation and Prerequisites

Doing beauty work for television, theater, or film is a feast-or-famine proposition. You're likely to be very busy or chronically underemployed. If you're a union member, you will be paid for your work by the hour. If not, you may be able to negotiate a per-project contract. Steady work can prove lucrative, but count on paying your dues for several years first. The best way to get started is to use your contacts to locate theatrical makeup artists in your community, and offer to assist them free of charge. (For television, contact the stations directly for the name of the hairdresser/makeup artist on the show you're interested in.) If you can get in the door and prove yourself competent, you're set. For more information on unions, see Chapter 6.

What Do Students Dislike about a Cosmetology Career?

Poor salary

Limited advancement

Long hours; working weekends

Angry customers

Boredom

Minimal benefits

Source: Procter & Gamble 1995 national survey,
"Who Are the Cosmetology Students of Tomorrow?"

Massage Therapist

This ancient art of muscle manipulation has experienced a tremendous renaissance over the past two decades. In fact, at the height of the dot-com era, it wasn't unusual to hear of companies hiring massage therapists to practice on stressed-out employees in the office. Massage was viewed as an important employee benefit and one that would help keep employees happy and sane. The popularity of massage has continued, and today we find more and more insurance companies covering massage as a treatment—a sure sign that it has become accepted by the masses. There are now as many types of massage as there are practitioners—Swedish, shiatsu, sports, reflexology, lymphatic drainage, Reiki, chiropractic, aromatherapy, craniosacral, polarity, and rehabilitative, to name just a few.

Some states require that massage therapists be licensed, and generally these licenses can be obtained either through a traditional cosmetology school or through a specialized massage school. Massage therapists can be employed by a salon, day spa, cruise ship, health club, or hospital, or they can have their own private practice at home, in conjunction with a salon, or in partnership with a medical practitioner such as a chiropractor.

Four factors above all others are key to success in this field:

▶ **Personality.** Your clients want to be soothed, not chattered at. A peaceful, serene presence is a must.
▶ **Talent.** You have to have good hands and practice makes perfect.

▶ **Location.** The area's residents must understand that massage is not only beneficial but also worth the cost.

▶ **Determination.** Stick with it and you will develop a solid following.

Compensation and Prerequisites

Most states require that you obtain a license to practice massage therapy. Then you might end up working in a salon, spa, doctor's office, health club, private practice—or even on a cruise ship. As the work environment varies, so does the compensation. A therapist may be paid a straight salary, salary plus commission, or commission only. A therapist in private practice will generally set his or her rates based on location and specialization. For example, if there are many practitioners offering aromatherapy massage in your area, then there is a fair amount of local competition and rates will reflect that. If you decided to practice Reiki, however, and there are no other Reiki practitioners within 150 miles of your business, then competition would be minimal and you might be able to charge a higher rate.

Sample Job Desciption #5
Shampoo, Styling, and Color Assistants

If you are a positive, outgoing individual who enjoys working with people, our upscale, busy salon and spa chain is hiring shampoo, styling, and color assistants to start in our training program. We have positions available in Dallas, New York City, and Napa Valley (in California). The job is full-time, working five days a week including some evenings and Saturdays. Schedules change from week to week. We require excellent communication customer service skills, in addition to a valid cosmetology license in the state in which you plan to train.

In the training program, you will work closely with our team of professional, experienced stylists and colorists. You will also be required to attend training on models every Thursday evening throughout this time frame.

If you are interested in working with us, forward a cover letter and your resume and qualifications to:

Human Resources Department
999 Greene Street, Suite 804
Dallas, TX 75228
214-555-5555
fax: 214-555-5555
e-mail: jobs@oursalon.com

School Instructor

Were you particularly inspired by one of your teachers? Do you want to share what you learned and how you learned it with others? Beauty schools always need dedicated teachers. A teacher can have a profound effect on a student's career. "I love watching my students learn and grow. It's my favorite part of the job. The time I devote to teaching has helped my own success as a salon owner because I invite many of my best students come and work for me once they've completed their studies. The first hair styling teacher I ever had gave me the same sort of personal guidance that I strive to give to my students today," says Miguel, who, in addition to teaching, owns and operates his own salon in Brooklyn, New York.

At Beauty Master College in Sarasota, Florida, a cosmetology teacher program teaches student instructors the psychology of learning, methods of teaching, lesson planning and preparation, classroom and school management, and Florida laws and regulations, in addition to providing supervised classroom teaching.

The biggest challenge facing teachers is burnout. "Teaching is extremely tiring," says Juanita Perez, a nail technician instructor at the Alabama Academy of Beauty. "I find that I work more hours a week than most of the people I know with regular 9-to-5 jobs. I spend much of the time I am not in class creating lesson plans, tutoring students, supervising students in the classroom, and grading assignments. You would think that being a cosmetology instructor is different from teaching most other subjects, but it's really just the same. I invest so much in my students and I find that this investment is returned to me ten-fold when I see them enjoying themselves in the classroom, motivated to teach others everything they have learned from me."

Compensation and Prerequisites

Most states require you to obtain an instructor's license, which can involve 200 to 1,000 hours of additional time in beauty school. Teachers receive a salary; yearly salaries run anywhere from $18,000 to $42,000, depending on experience.

Editorial Stylist, Nail Tech, or Makeup Artist

You can also combine jobs, working part-time in a salon, for instance, and part-time as the photo shoot hairstylist or makeup artist for a local advertising agency. You can also rent space in a salon and be your own boss.

Many people freelance in order to devote time to their own photo shoots. "Doing photo shoots really allows me to be creative in a way I can't be in my salon. Most magazines I work for want me to do something radical and different—I really get to test the boundaries of my creativity. Most of my regular salon clients would kill me if I did these crazy things to their hair," says Joanna Freeland, a freelance editorial stylist. Freeland got into doing shoots when one of her friends, Margie Rose, a fashion editor for a popular women's magazine, asked her to do a shoot for them. "I've done Margie's hair for years, so when her normal editorial stylist cancelled on her at the last minute, she called me, almost hysterical. From then on out, I worked regularly for Margie. Once I got my portfolio built and the word got out, my freelance career really took off."

Nail technician Marni Wells enjoys the change of pace she gets when doing nails on a photo shoot. "I really enjoy collaborating with the other stylists on a photo shoot. Once we sit down and start talking about the concept, my creative juices really get flowing. We all (the hair, the makeup, the nail artists, and other stylists) build off of each other's concepts. Someone will get a great idea for jungle hair and then the makeup artist starts thinking about jungle colors and I come in and give the girls camouflage nails. It's great fun working with other talented stylists who also see and understand your vision."

If you want to work in editorial, location is everything: New York, Los Angeles, and Miami are always important locations, but states like Montana and Oregon are seeing an increasing number of photo shoot crews, especially in the past few years since the urban cowboy look is in fashion. The important thing is to keep up-to-date on the industry and talk to people in the profession to find out how you can get started and where.

Compensation and Prerequisites

The biggest names in the hairdressing field—such as Frederic Fekkai, John Sahag, and Orlando Pitas—and the hottest makeup artists—Linda Mason, Laura Mercier, and Kevyn Aucoin—make tens of thousands of dollars per project. They are the exception. Generally speaking, advertising work pays more than editorial. If you really want to get your foot in the door, in addition to testing and building your portfolio, volunteer to assistant the big editorial names in your region. It's great exposure and education.

Sample Job Description #6
Spa Manager

Our Pamper Yourself Spa is open! We are seeking a dynamic spa manager to join our team. You must have a managing cosmetology license and management experience in a salon/spa setting.

The Spa Manger maintains the operation and supervises the spa room and associates. He or she generates sales, performs outstanding customer service, maximizes profits by controlling expenses, develops consultants, and trains associates.

Responsiblities include:

- Customer Service: Make sure that all associates adhere to customer service standards, ensure appropriate staffing levels, and deal with clients efficiently and politely.
- Sales Generation: Maximize business opportunities and focus on total store performance
- Merchandising: Create menu selection and product assortment, plan and execute floor sets and visual merchandising standards, and communicate ideas and suggestions to the General Manager and District Sales Manager to maximize business opportunities.
- Associate Development: Train, develop, and manage staff of cosmetologists, estheticians, and manicurists; motivate all associates to improve customer service performance; resolve associate issues and concerns, and maximize retention of associates; and ensure timely and accurate completion and administration of performance reviews for all associates.
- Communication/Interpersonal Skills: Develop and maintain effective, professional relationships with all levels of associates throughout the company and with customers, provide effective channels of communication within store.

Requirements

- Minimum three years experience in managing a day spa or salon
- Managing Cosmetologist License
- Must have strong customer service skills
- Excellent leadership skills required
- Retail background a plus
- Must be creative and innovative

EDUCATIONAL TRENDS

A set number of school hours—the number varies by state—are required before you can take a state board test to become a licensed cosmetologist. To obtain these credits, you must enroll in a licensed high school, community college, vocational/technical school, or postsecondary public or private school. In addition to these requirements, the states of Alabama, Kansas, Maine, Pennsylvania, and Rhode Island require you to hold an apprenticeship (the length varies by state) before you can take the exam. Apprenticeships are usually nonpaid, part-time positions in a professional salon.

Some states develop and administer their own state board exams; others use the exam established by the National-Interstate Council of State Cosmetology Boards. There has been a move in the beauty industry to establish universal national skills standards, but change is slow. The Cosmetology Advancement Foundation is currently developing a National Skills Standards Program, which identifies entry-level cosmetology skills standards that are accepted and supported by all segments of the industry. If adopted, the national skills standards will establish credibility for the industry and provide government understanding of the continuing need for licensure.

Once you pass your state boards, your education has only just begun. Most salons that accept newly licensed beauty-school graduates enter them into de facto apprenticeship programs that teach new graduates everything about the operation long before they are permitted to pick up a pair of shears.

Many smart salon owners require their staff members to participate in continuing education classes. These classes are usually held either at the salon or at a local distributorship on Sundays and Mondays (typically days off for salons) and are often taught by distributor or manufacturer education teams. They may be product-specific or generic. Such classes may be free, or they may cost your salon owner several hundred dollars. Regardless, they are to be taken seriously if you want to stay current—which is key to any cosmetologist's success.

Continuing education is available for a variety of specialties (not just hairdressing) and through a variety of sources. A motivational speaker may address you and your fellow staff members, or you may attend specific trade shows to broaden your knowledge. Consult with your employer to find out how to best go about this. Often, employers are happy to pick up all or part of the cost.

Bear in mind, too, that a number of states require you to complete a continuing education classes before you can renew your cosmetology license.

Employees hired right out of beauty school may need to go through a salon's training or apprenticeship program before they ever perform a facial or take scissors to a client's hair. During your early years in the salon, you will learn what it takes to build relationships with clients, how to behave and dress, and what's expected from you as a beauty professional, as well as all the new styles and techniques.

What Did You Like about your Former Cosmetology Career?

Helping people looking their best	51%
Working with customers	48%
Pride in the work	39%
Ability to be creative	28%

Source: Procter & Gamble 1996 national survey, "Why Do Stylists Leave the Salon Industry?"

As you continue in the process of becoming a beauty professional, your idea of which specialty is right for you may change dozens of times. One day you may love hairdressing, the next you might be convinced you want to become an esthetician, never to style hair again. If you begin with an open mind and remember that you are pursuing this career in part because you want to help others feel and look good, you may find that the specialty chooses you, rather than the other way around. In that case, you will be doing something you love—and what could be better than that?

THE INSIDE TRACK

Who: Victoria Anderson
What: Educational Programmer
Where: Pivot Point International, Inc.
                Chicago, Illinois

I can't remember wanting to be anything else when I grew up—I have always been interested in cosmetology. Even when I was little, I always gave all of my dolls haircuts and new hairstyles. Thank goodness I have gotten better since then!

I specialize in hair styling. I have worked in salons, but never rented workspace. My salon pay was commission-based. I now work for a hair and beauty education company. My employer offers health insurance and a 401(k). I did my basic training at Mueller's School of Beauty Culture, and I later took my teacher's training course there as well. I constantly take continuing and advanced education classes, and I work approximately 40–50 hours per week in my current position.

When I was job hunting, I let my friends and colleagues know that I was looking to change jobs, and tried to make contacts through them whenever possible. My advice to people just entering the field would be that every industry is a small industry, so make the most of everyone that you meet. Give back what you receive from others. Remember that you can learn something from everyone you meet.

During my first few years in this field, it was sometimes hard to admit that I still had a lot to learn about hair and the beauty industry. I've learned how important it is to be willing to offer the best customer service available, and work as hard as possible to build a clientele.

In terms of marketing myself, I used referrals almost exclusively. If my clients were happy, I knew that they would refer their friends and family to me. After five referrals, the original client was rewarded with a free service of their choice, so my clients had an incentive to send people to me.

As a cosmetologist, being able to make someone feel truly good about themselves is one of my favorite parts of work. I once had a client who had long salt-and-pepper hair. We had discussed cutting off most of her hair and donating it to "Locks of Love," a charity that makes hairpieces for children who have lost their hair due to illness. When she decided to do it, she arrived at the salon, quiet, kind of blending with the surroundings, not wanting to be noticed. I cut twenty inches off, gave her a short wispy cut, and applied a soft color to blend her gray. I sent her to have a complimentary make-up application. When she came back into the salon, her body language had changed completely. She stood up straighter, her shoulders back, her head up high, smiling. It was a great day for both of us! It's so rewarding to be able to help someone get a fresh look—a transformation on the outside can really change your feelings about yourself and your approach to life.

CHAPTER two

ALL ABOUT COSMETOLOGY EDUCATION PROGRAMS

BEFORE YOU can begin your successful career as a cosmetologist you need the necessary training. You need to build a foundation of basic skills, learn about trends in the beauty industry and how to stay on top of them, and develop the ancillary skills that will help you acquire your dream job. In this chapter you will learn what to expect from various education programs and how to determine what kind of training is best for you. You will get hints on how to maximize your education experience in preparation for a successful career. You will also find descriptions of training courses and tuition costs from schools across the country.

SO YOU'VE decided that you want to begin a career in the beauty industry. And, you understand that even if you are immensely creative, you still need to participate in a training program in order to be certified and licensed to work. It's best to start looking at your education options.

First, to practice cosmetology, you are required by law to pass a state board examination to gain a license. To take the state boards, you need to complete a certain number of class hours. The number of required class hours varies by state, but the requirement to pass a state board examination exists everywhere.

Second, you have many options when it comes to where you take cosmetology courses. You can take them at the public high school, public vocational/ technical school, public postsecondary (community college) school, or private postsecondary level. The postsecondary curricula generally take nine months to a year to complete, and those schools charge tuition; high school programs usually run two to three years and are free to qualified students.

If you take cosmetology courses in high school, you will be part of a small but growing number of students. The U.S. Department of Education National Center for Education Statistics *1998 High School Transcript Study* (June 2001) reports that there were 21,197 graduating seniors who had Cosmetology 1 on their graduate transcripts in 1998. That compares to 19,313 in 1994.

According to Gordon Miller, former president of Milady Publishing and now executive director of the National Cosmetology Association (NCA), private schools graduate, on average, about 65% of their students. Postsecondary vocational/technical schools and community colleges graduate between 40 and 50%, and high schools graduate about 20%. (That figure does not indicate that cosmetology students don't graduate from high school. Rather, it means that 20% of students complete the entire cosmetology curriculum.)

Miller attributes the fluctuating graduation rates mostly to motivation: "Students who pay money to attend a private institution are motivated to get the most out of their money. They've gone through the trouble to spend it, or to get a loan to cover it. They have more invested in it."

If you decide to start your training at the postsecondary private school level, your choices are many—there are more than 1,000 accredited private cosmetology programs across the country. (Accreditation is important because it means that the school is well-respected in the field, and also eligible for Title IV funding from the Federal Department of Education. For more information, see Chapter 3.) Since public schools don't charge tuition, financial aid isn't an issue, but some states do require that students complete their cosmetology education at the postsecondary level before they can take the state board exams. Additionally, many high schools don't have clinics or training salons available to students, so if you're participating in a high school program, it's likely that you won't get as much, if any, hands-on experience.

SkillsUSA—VICA (formerly Vocational Industrial Clubs of America) reports that cosmetology membership in the 2000–01 school year was 19,957 secondary and postsecondary; 18,406 at the high school level alone. They estimate that most of those cosmetology students participate in SkillsUSA—VICA programs that stress business, management, and people skills beyond basic cutting and styling techniques. Instruction in human resource management and interpersonal skills is important for cosmetology students because building a customer base is a big part of what makes beauty professionals successful. If you're interested in finding out which schools in your area offer SkillsUSA—VICA programs call 703-777-8810 or visit their website: www.skillsusa.org.

If you are a high school graduate and want to enter a postsecondary school, make sure that you thoroughly research your options before signing on to a particular program. Reading the information in this chapter will help you as you decide on the program that is right for you.

Sample State Requirements for Cosmetology License

Except as herein otherwise provided, the following shall be considered minimum requirements for license in the respective categories, and all applicants shall be of good moral character and temperate habits, be sixteen and a half (16½) years of age, have completed at least two (2) years of high school education or its equivalent, and:

As a registered cosmetologist:

Graduation from and completion of a two thousand (2,000) hour course of instruction in a school of cosmetology, or a four thousand (4,000) hour course of instruction as an apprentice covering all phases of the practice of cosmetology.

Successful passage of the examination for cosmetologist given under the direction of the board.

As a nail technician:

Have completed and graduated from at least a four hundred (400) hour course of instruction and graduated from such training in a board approved school, or an eight hundred (800) hour course of instruction as an apprentice in a specified cosmetological establishment under the direct personal supervision of a licensed cosmetology instructor, who shall have at least one (1) licensed nail technician on-site in the specified cosmetological establishment for each student being trained.

Successful passage of the examination for nail technician given under the direction of the board.

As an electrologist:

Have completed and graduated from at least an eight hundred (800) hour course of instruction and graduated from such training in a school approved by the board to teach electrology, or a one thousand six hundred (1,600) hour course of instruction as an apprentice in a specified cosmetological establishment under the direct personal supervision of a licensed electrologist instructor, who shall have at least one (1) licensed electrologist on-site in the specified cosmetological establishment as established by board rules.

Successfully passed the examination for electrologist given under the direction of the board.

As an esthetician:

Have completed and graduated from at least a six hundred (600) hour course of instruction for such in a school approved by the board to teach esthetics or a one thousand two hundred (1,200) hour course of instruction as an apprentice in a specified cosmetological establishment under the direct personal supervision of a licensed cosmetology instructor, who shall have at least one (1) licensed esthetician on-site in the specified cosmetological establishment for each student being trained.

Successfully passed the examination for esthetician given under the direction of the board.

Source: The Idaho Code

APPLYING TO AND GETTING INTO BEAUTY SCHOOL

Many schools look for students who have spent time in a salon, working as a receptionist, shampoo assistant, or in some other support role. In the application, show your creative side. The beauty industry can be very rewarding for people who consider themselves artistic but don't have an outlet for their creativity. The salon lets them have some creative freedom—without becoming starving artists.

If you've been through college or have a stable work history, play it up during your application interview. There is nothing an admissions officer likes to see as much as stability. A stable work history indicates that you're not likely to drop out of school and that you'll be worth the training time.

How much tuition is too much? High tuition can cause stress. However, if you want to go to a relatively expensive school and you qualify for a loan, you can make low monthly payments that continue over time. The bottom line: Upfront cost is an important consideration, but not as important as going to a good school in which you know you will be happy.

Sample Course and Hour Requirements

Here's a sample curriculum for a cosmetology degree program at Sampson Community College in North Carolina.

Title	Class	Lab	Credit
General Education Courses			
ENG 111 Expository Writing	3	0	3
Social/Behavioral Science Elective	3	0	3
Major Courses			
Required Core Courses			
COS 111 Cosmetology Concepts I	4	0	4
COS 112 Salon I	0	24	8
COS 113 Cosmetology Concepts II	4	0	4
COS 114 Salon II	0	24	8
COS 115 Cosmetology Concepts III	4	0	4
COS 116 Salon III	1	2	4
Other Major Courses			
COS 117 Cosmetology Concepts IV	2	0	2
COS 118 Salon IV	0	24	7
COS 150 Computerized Salon OPNS	1	0	1
Total Semester Credit Hours			**48**
Approved for Awarding Diploma			

Source: www.sampson.cc.nc.us/college/cosmetol.htm

Finding the School for You

The first and easiest place to start is to check the Yellow Pages for a listing of schools in your area. Take the search a step further by asking favorite salons in your area for recommendations. Also, don't forget to ask your hair stylist or nail tech where she went to school.

Once you have a list of potential schools, check the reputation of each by contacting about ten local salons and asking them for their opinions. You will learn a lot about the schools from what people in the industry say about them.

For instance, if they have never heard of a school, or don't say nice things about it, it's likely that the school is not the appropriate training program for you.

With your list of potential schools in hand, it is time to start the real evaluation process.

How to Evaluate Training Programs

Schools are businesses; they need students in order to make money. When you think about it this way, the brochure about a school is actually an advertisement. You, as a consumer, need to carefully research, evaluate, and compare schools the same way you would if you were buying a car or a major appliance.

Come up with a list of criteria for judging a school or training program's value to you. For instance, do you want to attend classes full- or part-time? Are you more comfortable in a suburban or urban setting? Is it accessible by public transportation? What kind of student-instructor ratio are you looking for? All of this information is available through a number of sources, including the schools themselves. Make a chart like the one below to help you compare the choices and make your decision.

My Criteria	School A	School B	School C	School D
Urban setting	X	X		
Public transportation	X	X		X
Clinic has public haircare services days	X			X
Student-to-instructor ratio less than 10 to 1		X		X
Financial aid offered through the school			X	
Career placement office and information	X	X		
12-month program or less		X	X	

Visiting Schools

After you have found a school (or more than one) that meets your criteria, you should arrange for a visit. Notice the people who attend the program. What are they like? Is the class schedule flexible? Look for choices in class schedule to accommodate your needs. What are the facilities like? Look for cleanliness and organization. Who are the instructors? Find out about the qualifications of the training staff.

You also can arrange to sit in for a day or two. This is called auditing. Spending some real class time at a school gives you a good idea of what your days would be like, what the students are like, and what the school is like.

Make sure you evaluate the curriculum. This is crucial; it reveals not only what you will learn but also how it will be taught to you. Check out course outlines and schedules. Also, look for a school that offers general business or career development classes—this information is invaluable for selling and marketing the techniques that you're learning about.

When you are there, be sure to examine the school's clientele. At the private school level, this isn't usually an issue, but public schools tend to attract clients who are elderly or on fixed incomes. If you are interested in practicing cutting-edge techniques, this clientele may not provide you with the best opportunity to do so. Try to find a program that advertises for clients at local colleges and universities. Students often lack the disposable income necessary to patronize expensive salons, but they are usually interested in current hair styles and trends.

Questions to Ask about Training Programs

Potential schools will make available to you pertinent information, such as the number of people who have attended the school, the number of people who have graduated, those who passed the state boards, and those who didn't. The state requires schools to track this information, so be sure to ask for it. Also, ask the schools in which you are interested in about their quality standards by inquiring about attendance requirements and academic performance requirements. This will tell you how serious the schools are about the education of the students, not just about collecting tuition. Specific questions that you will want to have answered are listed below.

1. **What are the fees?** You will easily find information on the tuition—it will doubtless appear in the school brochure or website—but what about the fees? What are they for? Are fees billed separate from

tuition? What's the refund policy? The financial implications of a particular program are important for you to consider up front.

2. **Is the program accredited?** The accreditation process recognizes schools and programs that provide a level of performance, integrity, and quality to its students and the community. It ensures that these schools conform to a minimum set of standards. The accreditation process is voluntary; accreditation is granted on the basis of the school's curriculum, staff ratios, and other criteria established by the accrediting agencies. Accreditation doesn't attempt to rank or grade the schools, only to accredit them.

   What does that mean to you? Basically, it assures you, and your potential employers, that the school you chose to attend tries to provide valuable courses taught by qualified, licensed instructors. In short, it offers you peace of mind.

   Most schools are proud of their accredited status and freely share the information in their printed materials, but you can be sure of their status by asking. You can also contact various accrediting associations to obtain a list of the schools they accredit and the standards they use. Some associations you can look into are The National Accrediting Commission of Cosmetology Arts and Sciences (NACCAS), the International University Accrediting Association, the Accrediting Commission of Career Schools and Colleges of Technology, and the Accrediting Council for Continuing Education and Training.

3. **What is the program's length?** You have several choices about the amount of time you spend on your training. Decide in advance how long you want to spend on your training and find a program that meets your needs and budget.

4. **What is the student-instructor ratio?** The student-instructor ratio is a statistic that shows the average number of students assigned to one instructor in a classroom or lab. It is important to know the ratio because a lower student-instructor ratio means that as a student you will get more small-group, one-on-one, intense training.

5. **What is the classroom-lab ratio?** The lab (also called clinic, practice, or working salon) experience—applying your knowledge in a hands-on environment—is at the heart of a cosmetology program. Evaluate how

much of your training time will be spent in the classroom versus the lab. A good program will have approximately a 1 to 2 classroom to lab ratio. This means that a program requiring 200 hours in the classroom would require 400 hours in the lab or clinic. Be cautious about any program that does not include significant lab work.

Although hands-on experience is key to any cosmetologist's success, some schools make the mistake of rushing students onto the floor too soon. Instead, look for a program that emphasizes both theory and practical instruction for the bulk of the required hours, and true salon work only at the end of the training.

6. **Is the school's lab up-to-date?** Investigate how the labs in your prospective schools are equipped, maintained, and updated. You need to be sure that you will be working with state-of-the-art equipment. If you are learning with equipment and materials that are out of date you will be way behind the curve when you begin your career. You also will want to ensure that the lab will enable you to practice on a variety of hair, skin, and nail types.

7. **What are the school's job-placement statistics?** Most schools and programs have specific placement offices dedicated to helping you find a job after you have completed your training. Placement offices keep records of what types of jobs their students get. Don't just read the statistics; closely examine them. For example, understand the difference between a statistic that shows how many students went on to full-time jobs in the beauty industry and one that shows all jobs, apprenticeships, part-time and full-time combined. Find out how many jobs were found through the placement office and how many students found jobs independently. Even if the school or program does not have a job placement service, you should be able find out what percent of graduating students find jobs in the beauty industry. Ask the admissions office for more information.

8. **What type of state board training does the school provide?** Look for a school that offers mock state board exams. This is an absolute must, particularly when you realize that the facials you learned about in week two aren't as fresh in your mind as they once were and that you could use a refresher.

Sample Curriculum

Here's an overview of the cosmetology curriculum at the Cosmetology Training Center in Mankato, Minnesota. The program consists of 1,550 hours (approximately 40 weeks) of instruction: 420 hours of theory, 980 hours of practical instruction, and 150 unassigned hours for special curriculum emphasis under the direct supervision of expert instructors:

Customer Relations (attitude, professional and business ethics, salesmanship, disciplines)

Theory Hours	25
Practical Hours	25

Cosmetology Laws and Rules

Theory Hours	15

(at least one hour per week during basic hours)

Sterilization, Sanitation, and Bacteriology

Theory Hours	20
Practical Hours	50

Anatomy (as related to cosmetology practice)

Theory Hours	45

Nail Technology (applied chemistry, applied anatomy and physiology of the human hand, fingers, and nails, including disorders and preventative measures and treatments)

Theory Hours	20
Practical Hours	50

Permanent Waving, Hair Straightening (cold waving, reverse permanents, applied anatomy and physiology of human hair, applied chemistry.)

Theory Hours	40
Practical Hours	150

Hair Coloring (bleaching, tinting, frosting and streaking, rinses, applied chemistry)

Theory Hours	40
Practical Hours	180

Personal Development (attitude, appearance, personal hygiene, poise, voice)

Theory Hours	50

Facials (makeup and arching of eyebrows, applied chemistry, applied anatomy and physiology of the human skin, problems of the skin, preventive measures and treatments)

Theory Hours	15
Practical Hours	30

Hairstyling (haircutting, geometric hair cutting and hair styling, fashion scissor cutting, waving curl construction, roller techniques, thermal [iron curling and pressing], comb-out techniques, shampooing [rinses], applied chemistry, disorders of scalp and hair, preventive measures and treatments, applied anatomy and physiology of the human hair and scalp)

Theory Hours	200
Practical Hours	400

Salon Management (salesmanship, business and salon etiquette, business ethics, employment practices)

Theory Hours	50
Practical Hours	25

Light Therapy (use of electrical equipment, safety precautions, high frequency current)

Theory Hours	5
Practical Hours	5

Unassigned Hours for Special Curriculum Emphasis

Theory Hours	150

Source: www.cosmetologytrainingcenter.com/cos_curriculum.htm

MAXIMIZING YOUR SCHOOL EXPERIENCE

Simply signing up for a training program is step one. It's important that once you begin expanding your knowledge base and skill set, you get the most out of the education available to you. Here are some tips for getting the most out of the training program you participate in:

Keep a Photography File

Even though you will be hard at work studying, it's still important to consider what you will need to do once you graduate. "Keep a photography file of your finished work as well as before-and-after pictures," recommends one stylist. You can create a portfolio from these pictures that will clearly document your accomplishments, skills, and special abilities. Combined with a professional resume, a portfolio can help you land the right job. Having a visual record of your work also will help you to see what your strengths and weaknesses are.

Set Goals for Yourself

Setting challenging, yet achievable goals for yourself while in school is essential to help you maintain your career focus. By thinking ahead and deciding what kind of salon you want to work in, you can focus your direction. Use the resources your school offers you. If your school offers courses in communication, take them. Salons will look for soft skills in applicants, and this training looks great on your resume.

Cindy Beecher of La' James Colleges of Hairstyling in Iowa and Illinois recommends working on your dependability. In a career in which knowledge constantly builds on itself, any time you interrupt the process, you're hurting yourself. "If you get into the practice of being tardy or missing a day a week, you will have problems," she says. "This is training camp for work." One goal you should set for yourself is to build the habits of a good employee.

Get Hands-on Experience

Take advantage of every opportunity to get hands-on experience. Use the lab as much as possible to fine-tune your skills. You're not limited to hours logged in the school's salon. Go on field trips to different salons and day spas to see how they operate, what their customer service is like, how their retail departments are set up, and how they book clients. Investigate any internship, apprenticeship, or assistantship programs your school may offer that enable you to get course credit for in-salon work. Employers will look at that as real in-salon experience, as well as note that you went the extra mile.

Take Notes in Class

Very few of us are gifted with a memory that allows us to retain all the information that bombards us throughout the day. Even fewer of us are gifted with a lightning-quick hand that can write down everything that is said in a classroom. So it is essential to your success in a training course that you use an effective note-taking method to help you learn and remember key information. Note-taking may not be practical in the lab or clinic setting, but in traditional classroom settings it is critical because your instructors will be imparting important information. Some types of note-taking methods are outlined below.

Traditional Outline

The traditional outline method typically mirrors the way that teachers will lecture. Concepts (broad ideas) are furthest out in the left-hand margin, marked by roman numerals (I, II, III, etc.); the ideas and details that expand the concept are marked first by capital letters (A, B, C, etc.); then Arabic numbers (1, 2, 3, etc.); then lowercase letters (a, b, c, etc.). Increase the indent with each level of detail.

You don't have to get all the lettering and numbering exactly correct. The important part of this method is to understand and accurately record the relationships between the ideas (example: Idea *A* is really a subset of that Idea *I*).

I. How to Make the Most of Your Training Program
   A. Taking Notes
      1. Outline
      2. Shorthand
   B. Studying for Exams

Invent Your Own Shorthand

Writing down every word in a lecture is virtually impossible. You will need to invent ways to abbreviate words. Constantly writing out *cosmetics* and *because* and *training* is just silly (and your wrist will protest). Just *bc* is sufficient for *because*. So many words end with *-ing*, why not just add *-g*? The common ending *-tion* can become *-tn*.

Drop as many vowels as possible without forgetting the meaning of the word. Therefore (and by the way, remember from science class that *therefore* is a triangle of dots?), *training* can easily become *trng*. Use acronyms (just the first letter of each word) for key terms that are repeated over and over. Do you know how many times I could write *n.t.* while you're spelling out *nail technician?*

You rarely need to write complete sentences. The meat of a sentence is its noun and verb—skip all the extra words (*the*, *it*, etc.). If you haven't tried it before, creating your own shorthand is going to take trial and error, just like any other note-taking method. Experiment with abbreviations while taking down information over the phone. Remember, it's not important that someone else understands your notes, only that *you* understand them.

Review Your Notes

Look over your notes as soon as possible after class—at least within 12 hours. Fill in any missing information that you still remember and cross out what obviously became unimportant by the time the class was done. Mark key points with a highlighter. Make sure each set of notes is clearly titled with date, course title, teacher's name, and overall theme.

Studying for Exams

Contrary to common practice, studying in a group or with your significant other is usually *not* a good idea. Human nature has a way of reverting to socializing rather than studying. Additionally, if you've perfected your note-taking skills, your friends won't understand the information you've taken in your personal notes anyway. Save your study time for weeknights and save your friends for weekends; that's how the work world is going to be, so you might as well get used to it. You will find that this is the most relaxing set-up of your time in the long run, even if it feels painful in the middle of the week. It will also prevent cramming for exams—pulling an all-nighter is *not* your red badge of courage in education; it's just plain ridiculous. Studies show that you will study less effectively and perform worse on the test when you are tired than when you are well-rested and alert.

So, set up a reasonably neat study area and make sure:

▶ Your lighting is good

▶ You have plenty of pens, pencils, Post-It notes, and highlighters

▶ Your telephone isn't going to ring with a tempting offer to blow off your study plans

▶ You have a comfortable chair and posture

▶ If you prefer listening to music while you study, that you're not going to be distracted by song lyrics or the awesome bass

▶ You have access to a computer that's connected to the Internet. You can use this as a powerful tool for research as well as practicing the hands-on skills you've learned.

Ask your instructor what the format of the exam is going to be: multiple choice, hands-on, or one of the many other methods of testing. You probably won't take many essay exams in your coursework; more likely you will encounter a lot of multiple-choice and lab (hands-on) tests.

Online Practice

Want some extra help studying for the state board? Try LearnATest.com's online practice cosmetology exam at www.learnatest.com.

If you develop good study habits during your training program, you will be well prepared when it comes time to study for the cosmetology exam.

Networking with Other Students

You will be meeting many new people in your training program—take advantage of this great opportunity. It's likely that there will be many students who are in more than one of your classes, and they probably have some similar goals and interests. During the lab portion of your training, you may be working very closely with some of your fellow students. Why not become friends with them and offer mutual support? It is also a good idea to compare with them what their course of study is and what they plan for the near future when training is complete. Note announcements of get-togethers for cosmetology students and attend with a friendly, open attitude.

Getting to Know Your Instructors

It is important to have peers for moral support and fun, but it's just as important to get to know your instructors. You will discover that professors and instructors are interested in your success. Once you've met one or two times in the classroom, find out your instructors' schedules and location of their offices. Make a point to drop by the office at least twice a month, even if it's just to chat about how things are going for you. Look for notices from student organizations announcing special social times to gather with instructors.

Sample Class Description #1

Cosmetology 1 (8 credits)—The student learns the techniques and procedures of haircutting, permanent waving, scalp treatments, shampooing, finger waving, pin curling, and hairstyling, together with blow-drying and thermal irons. Related theory is studied. The student is introduced to hairstyling for competition. In a laboratory setting, mannequin heads are used for practice work under the supervision of a licensed instructor. Occupational safety and sanitation, inherent in each procedure, are integrated and practiced. Professional image, communication and computer skills are integrated and practiced.

Making the Most of Your Career Placement/Counseling Office

Just think, there are squadrons of people out there who have made it *their job* to run career placement and counseling offices just for you! Take advantage of all their available services. Make the office one of the first places you visit when you set foot on campus, and include it on your list as you're doing rounds to the instructors' offices. Observe the posters and notices decorating the walls. Initially, ask a lot of general questions to get a feel for the office; then try to deal with only one person consistently with your specific questions. This will prevent you from becoming just a number—the same strategy you used in getting to know your instructors. If one staff person takes an interest in your situation, they will be able to give you more personalized help and more detailed information.

Not every placement office works in exactly the same way. Get to know the details of how your school's office works. Most offices participate in career fairs and distribute candidate position lists. Career fairs are a great opportunity to learn more about companies in the field and trends in the marketplace, get experience interviewing, and find a job.

Sample School Curriculum

The course of study is a two-semester program, beginning in the fall and ending in the spring. The one-year certificate program offered at Springfield Technical Community College follows the guidelines outlined by the Division of Registration, Massachusetts Board of Cosmetology. After passing the Massachusetts licensure examination, the student will receive a Massachusetts Operator's License. After two years of employment, the graduate may apply for licensure as a Cosmetologist with the Massachusetts Board of Registration in Cosmetology.

Semester 1

Class	Course Title	Credits
COSM-113	Cosmetology 1	8
COSM-116	Aesthetics 1	4
BIOL-146	Essentials of Human Biology 1	3
Total:		15

Semester 2

Class	Course Title	Credits
COSM-213	Cosmetology 2	8
COSM-216	Applied Aesthetics	4
SMBE-125	Introduction to Entrepreneurship	3
Total:		15

Source: www.stcc.mass.edu

STATE BOARDS

Once you've graduated from beauty school and met the minimum state requirements, you can apply to take the state board exam. See Appendix A for the listing, by state, of organizations that administer cosmetology exams. Contact them for information about the frequency and cost of exams, minimum age requirements, license fees, the number of applicants who passed the exam in the past year and the number who failed, licensing reciprocity with other states, and other questions you may have. Also contact them for further information on becoming a licensed board examiner in your state.

Making a Study Plan

Taking your cosmetology exam can be tough. Your career depends on your passing the exam. Even if you have graduated from your training program, if you aren't licensed, you can't practice cosmetology. The exam demands preparation if you want to achieve a top score. So, you need a study plan that will help you prepare. Follow these directions:

Step 1: Set a Time Frame

Allow yourself plenty of time to study and prepare for the exam.

Step 2: Get the Correct Information

Check filing dates for the test and double-check your information.

Step 3: Get All Your Materials

Find some review books or other materials you might need to prepare for the test. Try *Cosmetology Licensing Exam* (LearningExpress, 1998). If you have access to the Internet, you can find information online.

Step 4: Make a Study Schedule

Plan specific days and times to study and stick to your plan.

Step 5: Stick to Your Plan and Reward Yourself for It

Treat yourself to an afternoon walk, a candy bar, a long phone chat with a friend—anything that will reward you for maintaining a good study schedule. It isn't easy and you should pat yourself on the back when you can stick to your routine for some period of time.

Taking the State Board Test

The National-Interstate Council of State Boards of Cosmetology, Inc. (NIC), established in 1956, is a non-profit organization whose purpose is to encourage and maintain standards and requirements for entrance into and performance of the art of cosmetology and barber industry consistent with the need for protection of the health, safety, and welfare of the public. The NIC organization develops both written and practical exams for states' cosmetology and barber boards. In addition to providing very cost effective, standardized and reliable exams, NIC is the only organization that provides specific industry information to participating boards on the performance of candidates nationally, matters of sunset review, legislative issues, and the latest health and safety concerns.

The NIC board is composed of members of state boards of cosmetology or their counterparts in each district, state, or territory of the United States. To be a state board member though, you must be appointed by the state governor. Being involved as a state board member allows one to attend NIC regional and national conferences which are held in major cities throughout the United States, and to serve on various NIC committees including legislation, reciprocity, and health and safety. The experience gained at these conferences is a wealth of knowledge about industry trends, laws, and issues that make this profession so exciting.

All 50 states including Guam and Puerto Rico are members of the NIC, with a majority of states now on the NIC program. The advantages of having a national test is that it allows state-to-state reciprocity, whereby one can transfer the scores to another state and know the standards are identical.

In keeping the standards identical and up-to-date, the test development process becomes very important. Every five years a comprehensive national job analysis is conducted that involves thousands of practitioners and experts in various cosmetology- and barber-related occupations. In addition, continual psychometric and statistical analysis are conducted along with constant question rewriting and review to make sure the tests are accurately measuring the skills to be successful in the field.

NIC tests are developed in cooperation with Schroeder Management Technologies, Inc. and exceed testing industry standards as promulgated by the AERA (American Education Research Association), NCME (National

Council on Measurement in Education), APA (American Psychological Association), CLEAR (Council on Licensure, Enforcement and Regulation), and EEOC (Equal Employment Opportunity Commission).

"The changes in health-related issues and industry trends makes the constant review of questions even more important," says Aurie Gosnell, NIC founder and chairman of the test development committee. "Our goal is to make sure not only the public is protected, but the licensee as well."

Sample Class Description #2

Essentials of Human Biology 1 (3 credits)—This course, restricted to students in the Cosmetology program, presents an overview of human anatomy and physiology with an introduction to microbiology. Interaction of all body systems is discussed with emphasis on those topics relating to cosmetology. Specific topics included are cell structure, tissues, and the skeletal, muscular, and nervous systems.

Getting Ready for the Exam

A written exam basically has a right and a wrong answer, but a practical exam is a little more subjective, and thus more nerve-wracking. The judges of the practical exam are usually either state employees, state-contracted employees, or workers with a professional testing agency. Usually, they are certified by the state and are given specific task items to measure, such as, did the student measure whether the hair on both sides was even?

You will do well on each aspect of the exam if you:

► received a good education from a reputable school
► have good organizational skills—know where to start, what the next step is, etc.
► are good at problem solving
► think about the client during the practical
► know the material in Milady's *Standard Textbook of Cosmetology*
► try to relax

Sample Class Description #3

Applied Esthetics (4 credits)—The student will learn basic procedures of makeup and superfluous hair removal. Manicures, facials, and makeup procedures are part of this course and must be practiced in the lab under the supervision of a licensed instructor. Resume and portfolio preparation is integrated. Familiarity with a computerized test environment is gained as students prepare for licensure.

THE INSIDE TRACK

Who: Howard Kim

What: Salon Owner and Nail Technician

Where: Divine Nails, Beverly Hills, CA

I grew up in the 1970s and 80s in the San Fernando Valley with my older sister and my mother. My mother and sister would take me with them to the salon where they got their nails done, and I would sit and watch, transfixed. They mostly got basic colors, but my favorite thing to do when I was there was watch the nail technicians airbrushing nails, putting rhinestones on, and free-hand painting elaborate patterns and designs on ladies' fingers and toes. I asked the technicians endless questions about their creations, and I couldn't tear my eyes away. My mom had to pull me out of the salon when they were done.

By the time I was in junior high, my mom and sister didn't have to go to the salon any more. I had learned so much watching the technicians in the salon, that I could do almost anything, but I didn't have an airbrushing kit, so I had to freehand everything. I got really good with the tiny brushes, painting extremely intricate designs. By this time, my sister was in high school and all her friends started asking me to do their nails too. My mom's friends would come over and ask me to do their nails for special occasions. At first I just did it for free, but then, so many people started asking me to do their nails, that I began to charge money so that I could afford to buy my supplies, and I finally got an airbrushing kit.

It was really easy to keep up to date with nail trends just by reading magazines and chatting with the women who worked in salons in my area. Mostly, I came up with my own designs that seemed right for the personality and style of the women whose nails I was working on. Usually I did what just *felt* right, and the women loved it. My client base expanded rapidly when I was in high school—once girls found out that I did great nails. It was around then that I knew being a nail technician was my calling. I started saving up my nail money to put toward opening my own salon someday.

When I graduated, I decided to get licensed so that I could put my dream and my plan into action. I went to school and did my clients' nails on the side so that I was still making money and working toward my dream. At my school, I was the only male working toward a nail technician license. At first a lot of other students ostracized me, until they saw what I could do, and how much I knew about nails. Pretty soon, they started coming to me for help, and I began to feel more comfortable in the classroom setting.

When I finally got my license, I was able to work in a real salon, charge more for my services, and make more money. I still managed to keep a lot of the same clients I'd had since middle school, and I definitely gave them deals, but I wanted to make my dream of owning my own nail salon a reality. After about a year, I had enough money saved to lease a space in Beverly Hills. And that was just the beginning! I now own a high-end nail salon on Rodeo Drive. My client base has changed quite a bit—I have a large celebrity clientele—but I still do my close friends' nails and now I am in a position where I can do them for free!

My advice to someone who wants to be a nail technician is to be creative and follow your dreams. I think the fact that I was so focused on my goal for so many years helped me tremendously. It's definitely not been an easy road, especially since I don't know other male nail technicians. I've had to work really hard and be pretty resourceful to get to where I am now, but there's nothing better than doing what you love for a living, so you should see your dream through to the end.

CHAPTER **three**

FINANCIAL AID FOR THE TRAINING YOU NEED

IN CHAPTER 2 you learned how to find and succeed in the right training program for you. This chapter will help you pay for that program. You will learn about different types of financial aid and find information on how to gather your financial records, determine your eligibility for financial aid, distinguish between the different types of aid, and complete and submit your application. There are many types of financial aid available, and scholarships for which you may be eligible. The lists of resources and acronyms provided in this chapter will help you along the financial aid path.

YOU'VE MADE the commitment to pursue a career in cosmetology and you've decided on a training program. You understand that training is critical to your success but you might not fully understand the financial implications. Will you have to go into debt before you even begin? Not necessarily. If you are fortunate, perhaps your family has money to finance your training program, or you've been planning for a while and have saved the money yourself. If you are like approximately three-quarters of beauty school students, though, you will finance your education with some form of financial aid. With so many different types of financial aid available, there is a good chance that you can qualify for some aid, even if you go to school part-time.

Finding that aid and weighing the pros and cons of all of your options, however, can be confusing. This chapter aims to answer your most burning questions about financing your training program. Read through this chapter carefully and check out the many resources listed.

Also take advantage of the financial aid office of the school you've chosen, or your guidance counselor if you're still in high school. These professionals also can offer plenty of information, and can help guide you through the process. If you're not in school, and haven't chosen a program yet, look to the Internet. It's probably the best source for up-to-the-minute information, and almost all of it is free. Many cosmetology schools across the country have websites on which you can fill out questionnaires with information about yourself, and receive lists of scholarships and other forms of financial aid for which you may qualify. You can also apply for some types of federal and state aid online.

SOME MYTHS ABOUT FINANCIAL AID

The subject of financial aid is often misunderstood. Here are four common myths:

Myth #1: All of the red tape involved in finding sources and applying for financial aid is too confusing for me.

Fact: It's really not that confusing. The whole financial aid process is a set of steps that are ordered and logical. Besides, several sources of help are available. To start, read this chapter carefully to get a helpful overview of the entire process and tips on how to get the most financial aid. Then, use one or more of the resources listed within this chapter and in the appendices for additional help. If you believe you will be able to cope with your training program, you will be able to cope with looking for the money to finance it, especially if you take the process one step at a time in an organized manner.

Myth #2: For most students, financial aid just means getting a loan and going into heavy debt, which isn't worth it, or working while in school, which will lead to burnout and poor grades.

Fact: Both the federal government and individual schools award grants and scholarships, which the student doesn't have to pay back. It is also possible to get a combination of scholarships and loans. It's worth taking out a loan if it means attending the program you really want to attend, rather than settling for your second choice or not pursuing cosmetology at all. As for working while in school, it is true that it is a challenge to hold down a full-time or even part-time job while in school. However, a small amount of work-study employment (10–12 hours per week) has been shown to actually improve academic performance, because it teaches students important time-management skills.

Myth #3: I can't understand the financial aid process because of all the unfamiliar terms and strange acronyms that are used.

Fact: While you will encounter an amazing number of acronyms and some unfamiliar terms while applying for federal financial aid, you can refer to the acronym list and glossary at the end of this chapter for quick definitions and clear explanations of commonly used terms and acronyms.

Myth #4: Financial aid is for students attending academic colleges or universities. I'm going to a vocational training program, so I won't qualify.

Fact: This is a myth that far too many people believe. The truth is, there is considerable general financial aid for which vocational students qualify. There are also grants and scholarships specifically designed for students in vocational programs. The ACE (Access to Cosmetology Education) Grant, for example, is available only to cosmetology students.

GETTING STARTED

You will need a plan for financing your training. If you've already been in the workforce and plan to change careers, or if your parents have offered to pay for your education, you may already have the money you will need. There's no harm, however, in spending time investigating the financial aid and scholarship options available, even if you think you might not qualify.

Financial aid is available to cover the cost of education/training at several different types of schools, including vocational schools that offer short-term training programs. Chances are, you can qualify even if you're attending only part-time. The financial aid you will get may be less than that for longer, full-time programs, but it still can help you pay for a portion of your training program.

FINANCIAL AID 101

Now that you are convinced that you may be eligible for financial aid, you need to get a basic understanding of what financial aid is all about. There are many types of financial aid available to help with school expenses. They fall into three general categories: grants and scholarships, work-study, and loans.

Grants

These are awards that you do not have to repay. Grants are normally award-ed based on financial need. Even if you believe you won't be eligible based on your own or your family's income, don't skip this section. There are some grants awarded for academic performance and other criteria. The two most common grants, the Pell Grant and Supplemental Educational Opportunity Grant, are both offered by the federal government.

What's Out There

The Department of Education offers eight major student financial aid programs for post-secondary schools:

▶ Federal Pell Grants
▶ Federal Supplement Educational Opportunity Grants
▶ Federal Work-Study Program
▶ Federal Campus-Based Programs
▶ Federal Family Education Loans
▶ Federal Perkins Loans
▶ Federal Stafford Loans (subsidized or unsubsidized)
▶ PLUS Loans (Parent Loans for Undergraduate Students)

For information on these and other types of financial aid, call or visit the financial aid office of the school you'd like to attend. Ask for all the information available. Your public library reference desk can also help, and don't forget the Internet (but check out the accuracy of the sources of information you find there). In addition, there are entire books devoted to financial aid, many of which you can find at your local library.

Federal Pell Grants

Federal Pell Grants are based on financial need and are awarded only to undergraduate students who have not yet earned a bachelor's or professional degree. For many students, Pell Grants provide a foundation of financial aid to which other aid may be added. For the year 2001–2002, the maximum award was $3,125.00. You can receive only one Pell Grant in an award year, and you may not receive Pell Grant funds for more than one school at a time.

How much you get will depend not only on your Expected Family Contribution (EFC), but also on your cost of attendance, whether you're a full- or part-time student, and whether you attend school for a full academic year or less. You can qualify for a Pell Grant even if you are only enrolled part-time in a training program. You should also be aware that some private and school-based sources of financial aid will not consider your eligibility if you haven't first applied for a Pell Grant.

Federal Supplemental Educational Opportunity Grants (FSEOG)

FSEOGs are for undergraduates with exceptional financial need—that is, students with the lowest Expected Family Contribution (EFC). Priority is given in awarding FSEOG funds to students who receive Pell Grants. An FSEOG is similar to a Pell Grant in that it doesn't need to be paid back.

You can receive between $100 and $4,000 a year, depending on when you apply, your level of need, and the funding level of the school you're attending. There's no guarantee that every eligible student will be able to receive a FSEOG. Students at each school are paid based on the availability of funds at that school and not all schools participate in this program. To have the best chances of getting this grant, apply as early as you can after January 1st of the year in which you plan to attend school.

State Grants

State grants may be specific to the state in which you receive your education, in which you reside, or in which your parents reside. If you and your parents live in the state in which you will attend school, you've got only one place to check. However, if you will attend school in another state, or your parents live in another state, be sure to check them all; residency and eligibility requirements vary.

The ACE Grant Program

Established in 1997 through the joint effort of the Beauty & Barber Supply Institute (BBSI), the Cosmetology Advancement Foundation (CAF), and the Association of Accredited Cosmetology Schools (AACS), this program is designed to help schools recruit the kinds of students that salons have been clamoring for.

To apply for an ACE (Access to Cosmetology Education) Grant, simply stop by a local beauty school, call 1-888-411-GRANT for your application, or visit the Ace Grant website at www.ace-grant.org. You will receive a portfolio in the mail telling you about the program. In the portfolio are two salon assessment forms that you must then take to two local salons. The salon owner or manager will interview you and fill out the form, evaluating such things as your appearance, enthusiasm, suitability for a salon environment, and communication skills. You will then take these evaluations to the school you'd like to apply to, and the school will interview you as well. It's up to the school to decide whether to give you a grant; the ceiling on the grant is also up to the individual school.

Only AACS member schools participate in this program; find out if the school you've set your sights on participates by calling 1-888-411-GRANTS or visit the CAF website at www.cosmetology.org/ACE.html.

Scholarships

Scholarships are normally awarded for academic merit or for special characteristics (for example, ethnic heritage, parents' careers, area of study) rather than financial need. As with grants, you do not pay your award money back. You can obtain scholarships from federal, state, and private sources. Additionally, many schools have their own scholarship programs. Check out that option with your school's financial aid office.

The best way to find scholarship money is to use one of the free search tools available on the Internet. After entering the appropriate information about yourself, a search takes place which ends with a list of those prizes for which you are eligible. If you don't have easy access to the Internet, or want to expand your search, your high school guidance counselors or college financial aid officers also have plenty of information about available scholarship money. Also, check out your local library.

To find private sources of aid, spend a few hours in the library looking at scholarship and fellowship books or consider a reasonably priced (under $30) scholarship search service. Review the Resources section at the end of this chapter to find contact information for search services and scholarship book titles. Also contact some or all of the professional associations for cosmetologists; some offer scholarships, while others offer information about where to find scholarships. If you're currently employed, find out if your employer has aid funds available. If you're a dependent student, ask your parents and other relatives to check with groups or organizations they belong to for possible aid sources. Consider these popular sources of scholarship money:

Religious organizations
Fraternal organizations
Clubs, such as the Rotary, Kiwanis, American Legion, or 4-H
Athletic clubs
Veterans groups
Ethnic group associations
Unions

If you already know which school you will attend, check with a financial aid administrator in the financial aid department to find out if you qualify for any school-based scholarships or other aid. Many schools offer merit-based aid for students with a high school GPA of a certain level or with a certain level of SAT scores in order to attract more students to their school. Check with your cosmetology training program's admissions or financial aid office to see if they maintain a bulletin board or other method of posting available scholarships.

While you are looking for sources of scholarships, continue to enhance your chances of winning one by participating in extracurricular events and volunteer activities. You should also obtain references from people who know you well and are leaders in the community, so you can submit their names and/or letters with your scholarship applications. Make a list of any awards you've received in the past or other honors that you could list on your scholarship application.

A program benefiting mainly middle-class students is the Hope Scholarship Credit. Eligible taxpayers may claim a credit for tuition and fees up to a maximum of $1,500 per student (the amount is scheduled to be re-indexed for inflation after 2001). The credit applies only to the first two years of postsecondary education, and students must be enrolled at least half-time. Families whose adjusted gross income is $80,000.00 or more are ineligible. For more information on the Hope Scholarship Credit, go to www.irs.ustreas.gov/prod/forms_pubs/ or call 1-800-829-3676.

The National Merit Scholarship Corporation offers about 5,000 students scholarship money each year based solely on academic performance in high school. If you are a high school senior with excellent grades and high scores on tests such as the ACT or SAT, ask your guidance counselor for details about this scholarship.

You may also be eligible to receive a scholarship from your state (again, generally the state you reside in) or school. Check with the higher education department of the relevant state or states, or the financial aid office of the school you will attend.

Work-Study Programs

When applying to a school, you can indicate that you are interested in a work-study program. Their employment office will have the most information about how to earn money while getting your education. Work options include the following:

On- or off-campus
Part-time or almost full-time
School or nationally based
In the beauty services industry (to gain experience) or not (just to pay the bills)
For money to repay student loans or to go directly toward educational expenses

If you're interested in school-based employment, you will be given the details about the types of jobs offered (they can range from giving tours of the campus to prospective students, to working in the cafeteria, or other student-services offices) and how much they pay.

You may also want to investigate the Federal Work-Study (FWS) program, which can be applied for on the FAFSA. The FWS program provides jobs for undergraduate and graduate students with financial need, allowing them to earn money to help pay education expenses. It encourages community service work and provides hands-on experience related to your course of study, when available. The amount of the FWS award depends on:

When you apply (apply early!)
Your level of need
The funds available at your particular school

FSW salaries are the current federal minimum wage or higher, depending on the type of work and skills required. As an undergraduate, you will be paid by the hour and you will receive the money directly from your school; you cannot be paid by commission or fee. The awards are not transferable from year to year, and you will need to check with the schools to which you're applying: not all schools have work-study programs in every area of study.

An advantage of working under the FWS program is that your earnings are exempt from FICA taxes if you are enrolled full-time and are working less than half-time. You will be assigned a job on-campus, in a private non-profit organization, or a public agency that offers a public service. You may provide a community service relating to fire or other emergency service if your school has such a program. Some schools have agreements with private for-profit companies, if the work demands your fire or other emergency skills. The total hourly wages you earn in each year cannot exceed your total FWS award for that year and you cannot work more than twenty hours per week. Your financial aid administrator (FAA) or the direct employer must consider your class schedule and your academic progress before assigning your job.

For more information about National Work Study programs, visit the Corporation for National Service website (www.cns.gov) and/or contact National Civilian Community Corps (NCCC). This AmeriCorps program is an 11-month residential national service program intended for 18–24 year olds. Participants receive $4,725 for college tuition or to help repay education loan debt. Contact:

National Civilian Community Corps
1100 Vermont Avenue NW
Washington, DC 20525
1-800-94-ACORPS

Volunteers in Service to America (VISTA)—VISTA is a part of ACTION, the deferral domestic volunteer agency. This program offers numerous benefits to college graduates with outstanding student loans. Contact:

VISTA
Washington, DC 20525
1-800-424-8867

Student Loans

Although scholarships, grants, and work-study programs can help to offset the costs of higher education, they usually don't give you enough money to entirely pay your way. Most students who can't afford to pay for their entire education rely at least in part on student loans. The largest single source of these loans, and for all money for students, is the federal government. However, you can also find loan money from your state, school, and/or private sources.

You can get excellent detailed information about different sources of federal education funding by sending away for a copy of the U.S. Department of Education's publication, *The Student Guide*. Write to:

Federal Student Aid Information Center
P.O. Box 84
Washington, DC 20044
1-800-4FED-AID

Listed below are some of the most popular federal loan programs:

Federal Perkins Loans

A Perkins Loan has the lowest interest (currently, it's 5%) of any loan available for both undergraduate and graduate students, and is offered to students with exceptional financial need. You repay your school, which lends the money to you with government funds.

Depending on when you apply, your level of need, and the funding level of the school, you can borrow up to $4,000 for each year of undergraduate study. The total amount you can borrow as an undergraduate is $20,000.

The school pays you directly by check or credits your tuition account. You have nine months after you graduate (provided you were continuously enrolled at least half-time) to begin repayment, with up to ten years to pay off the entire loan.

PLUS Loans (Parent Loans for Undergraduate Students)

PLUS Loans enable parents with good credit histories to borrow money to pay education expenses of a child who is a dependent undergraduate student enrolled at least half-time. Your parents must submit the completed forms to your school.

To be eligible, your parents will be required to pass a credit check. If they don't pass, they might still be able to receive a loan if they can show that extenuating circumstances exist or if someone who is able to pass the credit check agrees to co-sign the loan. Your parents must also meet citizenship requirements.

The yearly limit on a PLUS Loan is equal to your cost of attendance (COA) minus any other financial aid you receive. For instance, if your cost of attendance is $6,000 and you receive $4,000 in other financial aid, your parents could borrow up to, but no more than, $2,000. The interest rate varies, but is not to exceed 9% over the life of the loan. The lender for these loans charges no fees, however, the borrower is responsible for two other fees. The U.S. Department of Education charges an origination fee of 3%, and the loan guarantor may charge up to 1% for a guarantee fee. Your parents must begin repayment while you're still in school and there is no grace period.

Federal Stafford Loans

Stafford Loans are low-interest loans that are given to students who attend school at least half-time. The lender is the U.S. Department of Education for schools that participate in the Direct Lending program and a bank or credit union for schools that do not participate in the Direct Lending program. Stafford Loans fall into one of two categories:

Subsidized loans are awarded on the basis of financial need. You will not be charged any interest before you begin repayment or during authorized periods of deferment. The federal government subsidizes the interest during these periods.

Unsubsidized loans are not awarded on the basis of financial need. You will be charged interest from the time the loan is disbursed until it is paid in full. If you allow the interest to accumulate, it will be capitalized—that is, the interest will be added to the principal amount of your loan, and additional interest will be based upon the higher amount. This will increase the amount you have to repay.

There are many borrowing limit categories to these loans, depending on whether you get an unsubsidized or subsidized loan, which year in school you're enrolled, how long your program of study is, and if you're independent or dependent. You can have both kinds of Stafford Loans at the same time, but the total amount of money loaned at any given time cannot exceed $23,000. The interest rate varies, but will never exceed 8.25%. An origination fee for a Stafford Loan is approximately 3% or 4% of the loan, and the fee will be deducted from each loan disbursement you receive. There is a six-month grace period after graduation before you must start repaying the loan.

State Loans

Loan money is also available from state governments. Remember that you may be able to qualify for a state loan based on your residency, your parents' residency, or the location of the school you're attending.

Questions to Ask Before You Take Out a Loan

In order to get the facts regarding the loan you're about to take out, ask the following questions:

1. What is the interest rate and how often is the interest capitalized? Your college's financial aid administrator (FAA) should be able to tell you this.

2. What fees will be charged? Government loans generally have an origination fee that goes to the federal government to help offset its costs, and a guarantee fee, which goes to a guarantee agency for insuring the loan. Both are deducted from the amount given to you.

3. Will I have to make any payments while still in school? Usually you won't, and depending on the type of loan, the government may even pay the interest for you while you are in school.

4. What is the grace period—the period after my schooling ends—during which no payment is required? Is the grace period long enough, realistically, for you to find a job and get on your feet? (A six-month grace period is common.)

5. When will my first payment be due and approximately how much will it be? You can get a good preview of the repayment process from the answer to this question.

6. Who exactly will hold my loan? To whom will I be sending payments? Who should I contact with questions or inform of changes in my situation? Your loan may be sold by the original lender to a secondary market institution, in which case you will be notified as to the contact information for your new lender.

7. Will I have the right to pre-pay the loan, without penalty, at any time? Some loan programs allow pre-payment with no penalty but others do not.

8. Will deferments and forbearances be possible if I am temporarily unable to make payments? You need to find out how to apply for a deferment or forbearance if you need it.

9. Will the loan be canceled ("forgiven") if I become totally and permanently disabled, or if I die? This is always a good option to have on any loan you take out.

APPLYING FOR FINANCIAL AID

Now that you're aware of the types and sources of aid available, you will want to begin applying as soon as possible. The first step is to obtain a copy of the Free Application for Federal Student Aid (FAFSA). The second step of the process is to create a financial aid calendar. Using any standard calendar, write in all of the application deadlines for each step of the financial aid process. This way, all vital information will be in one location, so you can see at a glance what needs to be done and when. Start this calendar by writing in the date you requested your FAFSA. Then mark down when you received it and when you sent in the completed form. Add important dates and deadlines for any other applications you need to complete for school-based or private aid as you progress though the financial aid process. Using and maintaining a calendar will help the whole financial aid process run more smoothly and give you peace of mind that the important dates are not forgotten.

The Free Application for Federal Student Aid (FAFSA)

This is the form used by federal and state governments, as well as school and private funding sources, to determine your eligibility for grants, scholarships, and loans. You can get a copy by calling 1-800-4FED-AID, or stopping by your public library or your school's financial aid office. Be sure to get an original form, because photocopies of federal forms are not accepted.

For more information, contact the Federal Student Aid Information Center (FSAIC) and ask for a free copy of *The Student Guide: Financial Aid from the U.S. Department of Education.* The toll-free hotline (1-800-4FED-AID) is run by the U.S. Department of Education and can answer questions about federal and state student aid programs and applications. You can also write to:

Federal Student Aid Information Center
P.O. Box 84
Washington, DC 20044

You can visit the FAFSA website at www.fafsa.ed.gov. This site will help you obtain and complete the FAFSA form. To complete this form, you will need the following information:

▶ Records for income earned in the year prior to when you will start school. (You may also need records of your parent's income information.) For the 2001–2002 school year, you will need 2000 information.

▶ Your Social Security card and driver's license

▶ W-2 Forms or other records of income earned

▶ Your (and your spouse's, if you are married) federal income tax return

▶ Your parent's federal income tax return

▶ Records of other untaxed income received such as welfare benefits, Social Security benefits, TANF, veteran's benefits, or military or clergy allowances

▶ Current bank statements and records of stocks, bonds, and other investments

▶ Business or farm records, if applicable

▶ Your alien registration card (if you are not a U.S. citizen)

To complete the form online using FAFSA Express, go to www.sfa-download.ed.gov/fafsa/fexpress.html. FAFSA Express makes applying online for financial aid faster and easier. The process automatically checks electronic FAFSA data, resulting in fewer rejected applications.

Getting Your Forms Filed

Follow these three simple steps if you are not completing and submitting the FAFSA online:

1. Get an original Federal Application for Federal Student Aid (FAFSA). Remember to pick up an original copy of this form, as photocopies are not acceptable.

2. Fill out the entire FAFSA as completely as possible. Make an appointment with a financial aid counselor if you need help. Read the forms completely, and don't skip any relevant portions.

3. Return the FAFSA before the deadline date. Financial aid counselors warn that many students don't file the forms before the deadline and lose out on available aid. Don't be one of those students!

When to Apply

Apply for financial aid as soon as possible after January 1st of the year in which you want to enroll in school. For example, if you want to begin school in the fall of 2002, then you should apply for financial aid as soon as possible after January 1, 2002. It is easier to complete the FAFSA after you have completed your tax return, so you may want to consider filing your taxes as early as possible as well. Do not sign, date, or send your application before January 1st of the year for which you are seeking aid. If you apply by mail, send your completed application in the envelope that came with the original application. The envelope is already addressed, and using it will make sure your application reaches the correct address.

After you mail in your completed FAFSA, your application will be processed in approximately four weeks. Then, you will receive a Student Aid Report (SAR) in the mail. The SAR will disclose your Expected Family Contribution (EFC), the number used to determine your eligibility for federal student aid. Each school you list on the application may also receive your application information if the school is set up to receive it electronically.

You must reapply for financial aid every year. However, after your first year, you will receive a Student Aid Report (SAR) in the mail before the application deadline. If no corrections need to be made, you can just sign it and send it in.

Common Financial Aid Process Mistakes

Simple mistakes could put your chances of receiving financial aid in jeopardy. Don't make these common mistakes:

Applying too late

Not reading instructions

Submitting an incomplete application

Using an incorrect Social Security number

Determining Your Eligibility

To receive financial aid from an accredited college or institution's student aid program, you must be a U.S. citizen or an eligible non-citizen with a Social Security number. Check with the Immigration and Naturalization Service (INS) if you are not a U.S. citizen and are unsure of your eligibility (1-800-375-5283/www.ins.usdoj.gov/graphics/index.htm).

Financial aid from many of the programs discussed in this chapter is awarded on the basis of need (the exceptions include unsubsidized Stafford, PLUS, and consolidation loans, and some scholarships and grants). When you apply for federal student aid by completing the FAFSA, the information you report is used in a formula established by the U.S. Congress. The formula determines your Expected Family Contribution (EFC), an amount you and your family are expected to contribute toward your education. If your EFC is below a certain amount, you will be eligible for a Pell Grant, assuming you meet all other eligibility requirements.

There is no maximum EFC that defines eligibility for the other financial aid options. Instead, your EFC is used in an equation to determine your financial needs. Eligibility is a very complicated matter, but it can be simplified to the following equation:

your contribution + your parents' contribution =
expected family contribution (EFC)

Student expense budget/cost of attendance (COA) – EFC =
your financial need

The need analysis service or federal processor looks at the following if you are a dependent student:

- ▶ family assets, including savings, stocks and bonds, real estate investments, business/farm ownership, and trusts
- ▶ parents' ages and need for retirement income
- ▶ number of children and other dependents in the family household
- ▶ number of family members in college
- ▶ cost of attendance, also called student expense budget, includes tuition and fees, books and supplies, room and board (living with parents, on campus, or off campus), transportation, personal expenses, and special expenses such as childcare

A financial aid administrator calculates your cost of attendance and subtracts the amount you and your family are expected to contribute toward that cost. If there's anything left over, you're considered to have financial need.

Are You Considered Dependent or Independent?

Federal policy uses strict and specific criteria to make this designation, and that criteria applies to all applicants for federal student aid equally. A dependent student is expected to have parental contribution to school expenses, and an independent student is not. The parental contribution depends on the number of parents with earned income, their income and assets, the age of the older parent, the family size, and the number of family members enrolled in postsecondary education. Income is not just the adjusted gross income (AGI) from the tax return, but also includes nontaxable income such as Social Security benefits and child support.

You're an independent student if at least one of the following applies to you:

▶ you were born before January 1, 1978
▶ you're married (even if you're separated)
▶ you have legal dependents other than a spouse who get more than half of their support from you and will continue to get that support during the award year
▶ you're an orphan or ward of the court (or were a ward of the court until age 18)
▶ you're a graduate or professional student
▶ you're a veteran of the U.S. Armed Forces—formerly engaged in active service in the U.S. Army, Navy, Air Force, Marines, Coast Guard, or as a cadet or midshipman at one of the service academies—released under a condition other than dishonorable (ROTC students, members of the National Guard, and most reservists are not considered veterans, nor are cadets and midshipmen still enrolled in one of the military service academies)

If you live with your parents and if they claimed you as a dependent on their last tax return then your need will be based on your parents' income. You do not qualify for independent status just because your parents have decided to not claim you as an exemption on their tax return (this used to be the case but is no longer) or do not want to provide financial support for your college education.

Students are classified as *dependent* or *independent* because federal student aid programs are based on the idea that students (and their parents or spouse, if applicable) have the primary responsibility for paying for their postsecondary, that is, after high school, education.

Gathering Financial Records

Your financial need for most grants and loans depends on your financial situation. Now that you've determined if you are considered a dependent or independent student, you will know whose financial records you need to gather for this step of the process. If you are a dependent student, then you must gather not only your own financial records, but also those of your parents because you must report their income and assets as well as your own when you complete the FAFSA. If you are an independent student, then you need to gather only your own financial records (and those of your spouse if you're married). Gather your tax records from the year prior to the one in which you are applying. For example, if you apply for the fall of 2002, you will use your tax records from 2001.

Filling Out the FAFSA

You will need the following documents:

U.S. Income Tax Returns (IRS Form 1040, 1040A, or 1040EZ) for the year that just ended and W-2 and 1099 forms

Records of untaxed income, such as Social Security benefits, AFDC or ADC, child support, welfare, pensions, military subsistence allowances, and veterans' benefits

Current bank statements and mortgage information

Medical and dental expenses for the past year that weren't covered by health insurance

Business and/or farm records

Records of investments such as stocks, bonds, and mutual funds, as well as bank Certificates of Deposit (CDs) and recent statements from money market accounts

Social Security number(s)

Even if you do not complete your federal income tax return until March or April, you should not wait to file your FAFSA until your tax returns are filed with the IRS. Instead, use estimated income information and submit the FAFSA, as noted earlier, just as soon as possible after January 1. Be as accurate as possible, knowing that you can correct estimates later.

Maximizing Your Eligibility for Loans and Scholarships

Loans and scholarships are often awarded based on an individual's eligibility. Depending on the type of loan or scholarship you pursue, the eligibility requirements will be different. EStudentLoan.com (www.estudentloan.com/workshop.asp) offers the following tips and strategies for improving your eligibility when applying for loans and/or scholarships:

▶ Save money in the parent's name, not the student's name.
▶ Pay off consumer debt, such as credit card and auto loan balances.
▶ Parents considering going back to school should do so at the same time as their children. The more family members in school simultaneously, the more aid will be available to each.
▶ Spend student assets and income first, before other assets and income.
▶ If you believe that your family's financial circumstances are unusual, make an appointment with the financial aid administrator at your school to review your case. Sometimes the school will be able to adjust your financial aid package to compensate.
▶ Minimize capital gains.
▶ Do not withdraw money from your retirement fund to pay for school. If you must use this money, borrow from your retirement fund.
▶ Minimize educational debt.
▶ Ask grandparents to wait until the grandchild graduates before giving them money to help with their education.
▶ Trust funds are generally ineffective at sheltering money from the need analysis process, and can backfire on you.
▶ If you have a second home, and you need a home equity loan, take the equity loan on the second home and pay off the mortgage on the primary home.

General Guidelines for Loans

Before you commit yourself to any loans, be sure to keep in mind that they need to be repaid. Estimate realistically how much you will earn when you leave school, remembering that you will have other monthly obligations such as housing, food, and transportation expenses.

Once you're in school

Once you have your loan (or loans) and you're attending classes, don't forget about the responsibility of your loan. Keep a file of information on your loan that includes copies of all your loan documents and related correspondence, along with a record of all your payments. Open and read all your mail about your education loan.

Remember also that you are obligated by law to notify both your financial aid administrator (FAA) and the holder or servicer of your loan if there is a change in your:

- ▶ name
- ▶ address
- ▶ enrollment status (dropping to less than half-time means that you will have to begin payment six months later)
- ▶ anticipated graduation date

After you leave school

After graduation, you must begin repaying your student loan immediately, or begin after a grace period. For example, if you have a Stafford Loan you will be provided with a six-month grace period before your first payment is due; other types of loans have grace periods as well. If you haven't been out in the world of work before, you will begin your credit history with your loan repayment. If you make payments on time, you will build up a good credit rating, and credit will be easier for you to obtain for other things, such as a mortgage. Get off to a good start by having a manageable budget, so you don't run the risk of going into default. If you default (or refuse to pay back your loan) any number of the following things could happen to you as a result:

- ▶ have trouble getting any kind of credit in the future
- ▶ no longer qualify for federal or state educational financial aid
- ▶ have holds placed on your college records
- ▶ have your wages garnished (withheld by the government to repay your loan)
- ▶ have future federal income tax refunds taken
- ▶ have your assets seized

To avoid the negative consequences of going into default in your loan, be sure to do the following:

▶ open and read all mail you receive about your education loans immediately

▶ make scheduled payments on time; since interest is calculated daily, delays can be costly

▶ contact your servicer immediately if you can't make payments on time; he or she may be able to get you into a graduated or income-sensitive/income-contingent repayment plan or work with you to arrange a deferment or forbearance

There are a few circumstances under which you won't have to repay your loan. If you become permanently and totally disabled, you probably will not have to repay the loan (providing the disability did not exist prior to your obtaining the aid). Likewise if you die, if your school closes permanently in the middle of the term, or if you are erroneously certified for aid by the financial aid office. However, if you're simply disappointed in your program of study or don't get the job you wanted after graduation, you are not relieved of your obligation.

What You Can Expect to Earn

Your earning power will depend on your location, type of salon, and whether you are paid a salary, salary plus commission (tips), or salary plus sliding scale commission. Having a general idea of what you may earn will help you decide how much you can afford to borrow and then repay at the end of your training program. The following U.S. average salaries are exclusive of commission (tips):

Manicurist:	$15,046
Electrologist:	$16,902
Hair Stylist:	$18,989
Barber:	$22,358

Source: Salary.com, July 2001

Loan Repayment

When it comes time to repay your loan, you will make payments to your original lender, to a secondary market institution to which your lender has sold your loan, or to a loan servicing specialist acting as its agent to collect payments. At the beginning of the process, try to choose the lender who offers you the best benefits (for example, a lender who lets you pay electronically, offers lower interest rates to those who consistently pay on time, or who has a toll-free number to call 24 hours a day, seven days a week). Ask the financial aid administrator at your college to direct you to such lenders.

Be sure to check out your repayment options before borrowing. Lenders are required to offer repayment plans that will make it easier to pay back your loans. Your repayment options may include:

Standard repayment: full principal and interest payments due each month throughout your loan term. You will pay the least amount of interest using the standard repayment plan, but your monthly payments may seem high when you're just out of school.

Graduated repayment: interest-only or partial-interest monthly payments due early in repayment. Payment amounts increase thereafter. Some lenders offer interest-only or partial-interest repayment options, which provide the lowest initial monthly payments available.

Income-based repayment: monthly payments are based on a percentage of your monthly income.

Consolidation loan: allows the borrower to consolidate several types of federal student loans with various repayment schedules into one loan. This loan is designed to help student or parent borrowers simplify their loan repayments. The interest rate on a consolidation loan may be lower than what you're currently paying on one or more of your loans. The phone number for loan consolidation at the William D. Ford Direct Loan Program is 1-800-557-7392. Financial administrators recommend that you do not consolidate a Perkins Loan with any other loans since the interest on a Perkins Loan is already the lowest available. Loan consolidation is not available from all lenders.

Prepayment: paying more than is required on your loan each month or in a lump sum is allowed for all federally sponsored loans at any time during the life of the loan without penalty. Prepayment will reduce the total cost of your loan.

It's quite possible—in fact likely—that while you're still in school your loan will be sold to a secondary market institution such as Sallie Mae. You will be notified of the sale by letter, and you need not worry if this happens—your loan terms and conditions will remain exactly the same or they may even improve. Indeed, the sale may give you repayment options and benefits that you would not have had otherwise. Your payments after you finish school, and your requests for information should be directed to the new loan holder.

If you receive any interest-bearing student loans, you will have to attend exit counseling after graduation, where the loan lenders will tell you the total amount of debt and work out a payment schedule with you to determine the amount and dates of repayment. Many loans do not become due until at least six to nine months after you graduate, giving you a grace period. For example, you do not have to begin paying on the Perkins Loan until nine months after you graduate. This grace period is to give you time to find a good job and start earning money. However, during this time, you may have to pay the interest on your loan.

If for some reason you remain unemployed when your payments become due, you may receive an unemployment deferment for a certain length of time. For many loans, you will have a maximum repayment period of ten years (excluding periods of deferment and forbearance).

Examples of Typical Payments for Perkins Loan Repayment

A borrower with a total loan amount of $3,000 will:

Have 119 monthly payments of $31.84 and a final payment of $28.90

Pay $817.86 in interest charges

Repay a total of $3,817.86

A borrower with a total loan amount of $5,000 will:

Have 119 monthly payments of $53.06 and a final payment of $49.26

Pay $1,363.40 in interest charges

Repay a total of $6,363.40

A borrower with a total loan amount of $15,000 will:

Have 119 monthly payments of $159.16 and a final payment of $150.81

Pay $4,090.85 in interest charges

Repay a total of $19,090.85

THE MOST FREQUENTLY ASKED QUESTIONS ABOUT FINANCIAL AID

Here are answers to the most frequently asked questions about student financial aid:

1. *I probably don't qualify for aid—should I apply for it anyway?*

    Yes. Many students and families mistakenly think they don't qualify for aid and fail to apply. Remember that there are some sources of aid that are not based on need. The FAFSA form is free—there's no good reason for not applying.

2. *Do I need to be admitted to a particular training program before I can apply for financial aid?*

    No. You can apply for financial aid any time after January 1. However, to get the funds, you must be admitted and enrolled in school.

3. *Do I have to reapply for financial aid every year?*

    Yes, and if your financial circumstances change, you may get either more or less aid. After your first year you will receive a renewal application which contains preprinted information from the previous year's FAFSA. Renewal of your aid also depends on your making satisfactory progress toward a degree and achieving a minimum GPA.

4. *Are my parents responsible for my educational loans?*

    No. You and you alone are responsible, unless they endorse or co-sign your loan. Parents are, however, responsible for the federal PLUS Loans. If your parents (or grandparents or best friend) want to help pay off your loan, you can have your billing statements sent to their address.

5. *If I take a leave of absence from school, do I have to start repaying my loans?*

    Not immediately, but you will after the grace period. Generally, though, if you use up your grace period during your leave, you will have to begin repayment immediately after graduation, unless you apply for an extension of the grace period before it's used up.

6. *If I get assistance from another source, should I report it to the student financial aid office?*

Yes—and, unfortunately, your aid amount will possibly be lowered accordingly. But you will get into trouble later on if you don't report it.

7. *Are Federal Work-Study earnings taxable?*

Yes, you must pay federal and state income tax, although you may be exempt from FICA taxes if you are enrolled full-time and work less than 20 hours a week.

8. *My parents are separated or divorced. Which parent is responsible for filling out the FAFSA?*

If your parents are separated or divorced, the custodial parent is responsible for filling out the FAFSA. The custodial parent is the parent with whom you lived the most during the past 12 months. Note that this is not necessarily the same as the parent who has legal custody. The question of which parent must fill out the FAFSA becomes complicated in many situations, so you should take your particular circumstance to the student financial aid office for help.

Financial Aid Checklist

——Explore your options as soon as possible once you've decided to begin a training program.

——Find out what your school requires and what financial aid they offer.

——Complete and mail the FAFSA as soon as possible after January 1st.

——Complete and mail other applications by the deadlines.

——Gather loan application information and forms from your college financial aid office.

——Carefully read all letters and notices from the school, the federal student aid processor, the need analysis service, and private scholarship organizations. Note whether financial aid will be sent before or after you are notified about admission, and how exactly you will receive the money.

——Report any changes in your financial resources or expenses to your financial aid office so they can adjust your award accordingly.

——Re-apply each year.

Financial Aid Acronyms Key

COA	Cost of Attendance
CWS	College Work-Study
EFC	Expected Family Contribution
EFT	Electronic Funds Transfer
ESAR	Electronic Student Aid Report
ETS	Educational Testing Service
FAA	Financial Aid Administrator
FAF	Financial Aid Form
FAFSA	Free Application for Federal Student Aid
FAO	Financial Aid Office
FDSLP	Federal Direct Student Loan Program
FFELP	Federal Family Education Loan Program
FSEOG	Federal Supplemental Educational Opportunity Grant
FWS	Federal Work-Study
GSL	Guaranteed Student Loan
PC	Parent Contribution
PLUS	Parent Loan for Undergraduate Students
SAP	Satisfactory Academic Progress
SC	Student Contribution
USED	U.S. Department of Education

FINANCIAL AID TERMS—CLEARLY DEFINED

Accrued interest—Interest that accumulates on the unpaid principal balance of your loan.

Capitalization of interest—Addition of accrued interest to the principal balance of your loan that increases both your total debt and monthly payments.

Default (you won't need this one, right?)—Failure to repay your education loan.

Deferment—A period when a borrower, who meets certain criteria, may suspend loan payments.

Delinquency (you won't need this one, either!)—Failure to make payments when due.

Disbursement—Loan funds issued by the lender.

Forbearance—Temporary adjustment to repayment schedule for cases of financial hardship.

Grace period—Specified period of time after you graduate or leave school during which you need not make payments.

Holder—The institution that currently owns your loan.

In-school grace and **deferment interest subsidy**—Interest the federal government pays for borrowers on some loans while the borrower is in school, during authorized deferments, and during grace periods.

Interest—Cost you pay to borrow money.

Interest-only payment—A payment that covers only interest owed on the loan and none of the principal balance.

Lender (Originator)—Puts up the money when you take out a loan. Most lenders are financial institutions, but some state agencies and schools make loans too.

Origination fee—Fee, deducted from the principal, which is paid to the federal government to offset its cost of the subsidy to borrowers under certain loan programs.

Principal—Amount you borrow, which may increase as a result of capitalization of interest, and the amount on which you pay interest.

Promissory note—Contract between you and the lender that includes all the terms and conditions under which you promise to repay your loan.

Secondary markets—Institutions that buy student loans from originating lenders, thus providing lenders with funds to make new loans.

Servicer—Organization that administers and collects your loan. May be either the holder of your loan or an agent acting on behalf of the holder.

Subsidized Stafford Loans—Loans based on financial need. The government pays the interest on a subsidized Stafford Loan for borrowers while they are in school and during specified deferment periods.

Unsubsidized Stafford Loans—Loans available to borrowers, regardless of family income. Unsubsidized Stafford Loan borrowers are responsible for the interest while in school, deferment periods, and repayment.

FINANCIAL AID RESOURCES

In addition to the sources listed throughout this chapter, these are additional resources that may be used to obtain more information about financial aid.

Telephone Numbers

Federal Student Aid Information Center	800-4-FED-AID
(U.S. Department of Education) Hotline	800-433-3243
TDD Number for Hearing-Impaired	800-730-8913
For suspicion of fraud or abuse	800-MIS-USED
of federal aid	(800-647-8733)
Selective Service	847-688-6888
Immigration and Naturalization (INS)	415-705-4205
Internal Revenue Service (IRS)	800-829-1040
Social Security Administration	800-772-1213
National Merit Scholarship Corporation	708-866-5100
Sallie Mae's college AnswerSM Service	800-222-7183
Career College Association	202-336-6828
ACT: American College Testing program	916-361-0656
(about forms submitted to the need analysis servicer)	
College Scholarship Service (CSS)	609-771-7725; TDD 609-883-7051
Need Access/Need Analysis Service	800-282-1550
FAFSA on the WEB Processing/ Software Problems	800-801-0576

Websites

Using any Internet search engine, such as Google (www.google.com) or Dogpile (www.dogpile.com), use the search phrase "Financial Aid" or "Cosmetology Scholarship" to gain access to a wide selection of online-based resources relating to scholarships, loans, lending organizations, and financial planning. Here are some websites that offer general financial aid information:

www.ed.gov\prog_info\SFA\FAFSA
This site offers students help in completing the FAFSA.

www.ed.gov/offices/OPE/t4_codes.html
This site offers a list of Title IV school codes that you may need to complete the FAFSA.

www.ed.gov/offices/OSFAP/Students/apply/express.html
This site enables you to fill out and submit the FAFSA online. You will need to print out, sign, and send in the release and signature pages.

www.finaid.org
This site has many pages addressing special situations, such as bankruptcy, defaulting on student loans, divorced parents, financially unsupportive parents, and myths about financial aid.

www.fastweb.com
If you answer a few simple questions (such as geological location and age), you will receive a list of scholarships for which you may qualify. Their database is updated regularly, and your list will be updated when new scholarships are added that fit your profile.

www.career.org
This is the website of the Career College Association (CCA). It offers a limited number of scholarships for attendance at private proprietary schools. You can also contact CCA at 750 First Street, NE, Suite 900, Washington, DC 20002-4242.

www.salliemae.com
Website for the Sallie Mae (Student Loan Marketing Association) that contains information about loan programs.

www.wiredscholar.com
This site, a service of Sallie Mae, has useful tools and information that can help you with the entire process of financing your training program. The affordability analyzers are particularly helpful.

www.fedmoney.org
This site explains everything from the application process (you can actually download the applications you will need), eligibility requirements and the different types of loans available.

Software Programs

Cash for Class
Tel: 800-205-9581
Fax: 714-673-9039

Redheads Software, Inc.
3334 East Coast Highway #216
Corona del Mar, CA 92625
e-mail: cashclass@aol.com

C-LECT Financial Aid Module
Chronicle Guidance Publications
P.O. Box 1190
Moravia, NY 13118-1190
Tel: 800-622-7284 or 315-497-0330
Fax: 315-497-3359

Peterson's Award Search
Peterson's
P.O. Box 2123
Princeton, NJ 08543-2123
800-338-3282 or 609-243-9111
e-mail: custsvc@petersons.com

**Pinnacle Peak Solutions
(Scholarships 101)**
Pinnacle Peak Solutions
7735 East Windrose Drive
Scottsdale, AZ 85260
800-762-7101 or 602-951-9377
Fax: 602-948-7603

**TP Software—Student Financial
Aid Search Software**
TP Software
P.O. Box 532
Bonita, CA 91908-0532
800-791-7791 or 619-496-8673
e-mail: mail@tpsoftware.com

Books and Pamphlets

The Student Guide. Published by the U.S. Department of Education, this is the handbook about federal aid programs. To get a printed copy, call 1-800-4FED-AID.

Looking for Student Aid. Published by the U.S. Department of Education, this is an overview of sources of information about financial aid. To get a printed copy, call 1-800-4FED-AID.

How Can I Receive Financial Aid for College? Published from the Parent Brochures ACCESS ERIC website. Order a printed copy by calling 1-800-LET-ERIC or write to ACCESS ERIC, Research Blvd-MS 5F, Rockville, MD 20850-3172.

Cassidy, David J. *The Scholarship Book 2002: The Complete Guide to Private-Sector Scholarships, Fellowships, Grants, and Loans for the Undergraduate.* (Englewood Cliffs, NJ: Prentice Hall, 2001).

Chany, Kalman A. and Geoff Martz. *Student Advantage Guide to Paying for College 1997 Edition.* (New York: The Princeton Review, 1997.)

College Costs & Financial Aid Handbook, 18th ed (New York: The College Entrance Examination Board, 1998).

Cook, Melissa L. *College Student's Handbook to Financial Assistance and Planning* (Traverse City, MI: Moonbeam Publications, Inc., 1991).

Davis, Kristen. *Financing College: How to Use Savings, Financial Aid, Scholarships, and Loans to Afford the School of Your Choice* (Washington, DC: Random House, 1996).

Davis, Herm and Joyce Lain Kennedy. *College Financial Aid for Dummies* (Foster City, CA: IDG Books Worldwide, 1999).

Peterson's Scholarships, Grants and Prizes 2002 (Princeton, NJ: Peterson's, 2001).

Ragins, Marianne. *Winning Scholarships for College: An Insider's Guide* (New York: Henry Holt, 1994).

Scholarships, Grants & Prizes: Guide to College Financial Aid from Private Sources. (Princeton, NJ: Peterson's, 1998).

Schwartz, John. *College Scholarships and Financial Aid* (New York: Simon & Schuster, Macmillan, 1995).

Schlacter, Gail and R. David Weber. *Scholarships 2000* (New York: Kaplan, 1999).

To find additional books, you may want to visit an online bookseller such as Barnes & Noble (www.bn.com) or Amazon.com (www.amazon.com). There you can enter any search phrase that is appropriate to what you are looking for.

Other Related Financial Aid Books

Annual Register of Grant Support (Chicago, IL: Marquis, Annual).

A's and B's of Academic Scholarships (Alexandria, VA: Octameron, Annual).

Chronicle Student Aid Annual (Moravia, NY: Chronicle Guidance, Annual).

College Blue Book. Scholarships, Fellowships, Grants and Loans (New York: Macmillan, Annual).

College Financial Aid Annual (New York: Prentice Hall, Annual).

Directory of Financial Aids for Minorities (San Carlos, CA: Reference Service Press, Biennial).

Directory of Financial Aids for Women (San Carlos, CA: Reference Service Press, Biennial).

Financial Aids for Higher Education (Dubuque: Wm. C. Brown, Biennial).

Financial Aid for the Disabled and their Families (San Carlos, CA: Reference Service Press, Biennial).

Leider, Robert and Ann. *Don't Miss Out: the Ambitious Student's Guide to Financial Aid* (Alexandria, VA: Octameron, Annual).

Paying Less for College (Princeton, NJ: Peterson's Guides, Annual).

THE INSIDE TRACK

Who: Kathy Kafka

What: Educator

Where: Zotos International,
             Chicago, Illinois

I first learned about cosmetology through my brother's girlfriend, who had worked her way through college as a cosmetologist. Originally, I wanted to be a grade school teacher. Because the hours are so flexible, I realized that cosmetology would allow me to go to teaching school and also work full time. I thought I would go to cosmetology school full time for nine months, and then start college the following fall. Instead I became more involved with the industry and learned about the great opportunities it had to offer. That was 32 years ago, and I'm still working in the industry—active and always learning.

I attended a local cosmetology school, which was a 1,500-hour (2-term) course. I also completed an additional 1,000 hours to obtain a teacher's license. I live in Illinois, which requires cosmetology professionals to take continuing education courses in order to renew our licenses. This is not a requirement in all states, but I'm a firm believer in education, so I happily take on the course work. We work in an industry that is always changing, and to keep up-to-date we must continue to learn and grow.

The first year, trying to get established was the most challenging time for me. Building a clientele takes time. It can be difficult to maintain your enthusiasm during the long hours and hard work, but it does pay off.

I've had a number of jobs within the industry. I've worked as a stylist, manager and owner of a salon, educator, platform artist, and now regional education manager. When I found this position, I was at a point in my career when I needed a change. I had worked in a salon as a stylist, manager, and owner. I worked as a teacher and was looking for a new challenge. I sent my resume to some large manufacturers, and was fortunate enough to be hired three weeks later.

I now work as an educator for a manufacturing company that produces professional hair care products and perm solutions, and I'm also a licensed instructor of cosmetology. I am salaried, and my company offers healthcare, life insurance, and 401(k).

Much of the networking I did while job-hunting was through Cosmetologists Chicago, which is an affiliate of the National Cosmetology Association. By being a member, not only do I receive continuing education, but I've met numerous stylists, nail techs, estheticians, and owners. These contacts have been useful to me professionally, but I've also made lifetime friends.

When I worked in the salon, I promoted myself by word of mouth. When a client referred someone to me, I would send a small arrangement of flowers to their work place as a thank-you. My clients appreciated it, and the flowers also generated conversation and questions, often sending another client my way.

In my current position, I've had the opportunity to travel in all 50 states, as well as internationally. I conduct in-salon training sessions, as well as training at distributor and trade shows. My job allows me access to products when they are in the development stages, so I have input with the chemist on a regular basis.

I think most people think of cosmetology as just standing behind a chair. Yes, some of it is that, and I enjoy the personal contact with my clients. But there is so much more. I have friends who work in the theater, for television and movies, on cruise ships, and as platform artists and sales consultants. It's a field that is filled with opportunity—Get out there and take advantage of it!

CHAPTER four

HOW TO LAND YOUR FIRST JOB

THE ALL-IMPORTANT first job. You've been dreaming about it ever since you decided to become a beauty professional. Now you're ready to go for it! In this chapter you will learn what you need to do to land your first job—the job you really want. You will find practical tips on how to get job-related information and how to conduct your search.

A JOB search can be a stressful time. After all, you will be spending up to 40 hours or more at your job each week, so you will want to be sure that it is the one for you. With many factors to consider during your job search, it can become overwhelming. The easiest way to minimize stress and conduct a successful job search is to prepare and be organized. This method helped you when you were searching for a beauty school, and it will help you now as you embark on the road to career success.

If you don't already have one (and you should because they are indispensable for students as well as professionals), purchase a daily planner. The type and style is up to you, just be sure that you feel comfortable using it. Some people like a notebook style that reveals a full month on a two-page spread, some people like to see one week per page, or even one day per page.

Or, you can be up-to-the-minute and purchase an electronic device, such as a Palm Pilot™.

The planner will be essential for helping you keep track of when you sent letters and resumes, made phone calls, and set up interviews. You can also use it to maintain your list of contacts—people you have met during while networking who may help you find a job. And, keep your to-do list here. This way, everything vital to your job search is in one place.

DEVELOPING YOUR PLAN

In order to find the perfect job, you need to evaluate both your short-term and long-term career goals. You've gotten a taste of the salon life at beauty school; now it's time to explore those possibilities more fully. To get the job you want, you need to:

- ▶ know the kind of job you want
- ▶ conduct a job search
- ▶ develop a resume
- ▶ polish your cover letter-writing skills
- ▶ put together a portfolio
- ▶ learn how to give a great interview
- ▶ understand which benefits are priorities for you
- ▶ know your career options

You don't need to have all of the answers now—you just need to know what you should think about at the start of the process. You may decide to specialize in hair color rather than cutting somewhere down the road; you may learn that teaching is what you'd most like to do; or you may find out that management, not creative work, is what strikes your fancy. Rare is the individual who knows exactly what he or she wants at the very beginning of his or her career. Don't panic. There should be plenty of time, room, and opportunity to explore your options. You will want your first job to further your long-term objective, however loose or unformed that objective may be.

To develop an objective that will give your job search a focus and reduce your job search stress, here are some questions for you to consider as you start out:

► Which classes did you like the most in beauty school?

► Which classes did you like the least?

► Are you looking for a flexible or set schedule?

► Do you want to work full- or part-time?

► Do you want to work in a large spa environment or a small salon?

► Are you willing to relocate to find a job?

► How long of a commute are you willing to make?

► Which benefits are important to you?
>   ► Health
>   ► Dental
>   ► Vision
>   ► 401(k)
>   ► Vacation

► Do you foresee yourself becoming a salon manager or owner in the future?

The answers to these questions will tell you a lot about the type of job you should look for.

WHERE THE ENTRY-LEVEL JOBS ARE

Where can you expect to be working at the end of your job search? That depends on a number of different factors, including what your career objective is, where you are located, what type of physical environment you believe you will thrive in, and others. It will help you to know where the jobs are as you go through the job search process. You will find that is it easier to look for a job when you know what you are looking for. For example, there are many entry-level jobs in salons, spas, department stores, cruise ships, and hotels. There are fewer entry-level jobs as makeup artists for the TV and film industry. For a job in that industry, you will need to gain experience (volunteering your services for community theater and documenting your skills in your portfolio, for example) or you can try to find a professional who will hire you as an assistant.

Similarly, you may find that the best route to your perfect job is through an apprenticeship. As an apprentice, you will gradually gain more experience as you prove yourself capable of handling it.

Salon Stats

According to the most recent data available from the National Accrediting Commission of Cosmetology Arts and Sciences (NACCAS), there are 1,286,000 licensed professionals employed in the nation's 296,563 beauty salons, barber shops, unisex salons, and nail salons. The typical salon serves 174 clients per week and has five stations, two or three full-time professionals, one part-time professional, and one booth renter. Approximately three out of four salon owners reported difficulty in finding new applicants—good news for entry-level professionals.

There is a great deal of mobility in the industry. One out of every three salon employees changed jobs last year, creating over 419,000 filled job openings or 1.4 openings per establishment. Considering that half of the establishments have one to three people, this is an enormous turnover rate. Employees most often leave to work in other salon establishments (19%). Nearly 10% left to open their own establishment and 15% left to become booth renters.

The salon industry continues to be a job-seekers market. Salon owners report that they planned on filling 500,000 positions in the first six months of 1999. Approximately three out of every four salon owners who looked for new employees in 1998 reported difficulty in finding qualified personnel. Employment prospects are good for those interested in reentering the field and for recent cosmetology program graduates. Some 43% of employees leaving their current position leave to go back to school, raise a family, or work in an unrelated industry. Thus, there were approximately 180,000 positions for recent graduates and re-entrants; over 100,000 of those positions were filled in 1998 with people with less than one year of experience.

Other key findings:

- 70% of salon owners classified their salon as a full-service salon, 13% as a haircutting salon, 4% as a nail salon, and 9% as a barber shop.
- 60% of salon employees work full-time, 29% are part-time (20–35 hours), and 11% are low-time (less than 20 hours).
- The average salon income, including tips, figures to be about $18.50/hour.
- While manicurists are currently only 2.6% of the current industry employees, some 21% of the anticipated vacancies are for professionals with those skills.

Source: "Key Findings of the 1999 Job Demand Survey"
(www.naccas.org/Press-Release/NaccasNews/JobDemand_survey.htm)

Number of Anticipated Job Openings, January–June 1999

	Northeast	South	N. Central	West
Cosmetologists	33,571	103,905	50,325	49,790
Barber/Stylists	12,641	27,759	8,799	10,270
Skin Care Specialists	3,100	6,928	2,988	4,928
Electrologists	579	1,009	321	913
Nail Technician	14,206	56,877	15,030	18,434
Assistant Stylist	10,072	9,454	5,956	3,103
Massage Therapist	3,934	9,313	4,106	5,475
Aestheticians	2,199	4,269	1,278	3,833
Total	82,881	225,948	90,564	98,388

Source: "Job Demand in the Cosmetology Industry, 1999," a national survey conducted for the National Accrediting Commission of Cosmetology Arts and Sciences (NACCAS).

RESEARCHING EMPLOYERS

You select a restaurant based on decor, atmosphere, and of course, food quality. You should research your first cosmetology job in a similar manner. When considering a salon, make sure it is clean, has well-stocked shelves of professional retail products, and is considered established among salons in the area. Notice if the cosmetologists are up on current trends and technology. A salon should have a good marketing strategy, too. This shows that the owner and the staff are making an effort to retain clients, to get new clients, and to promote the services and products of the salon.

Successful, established salons offer higher job security because they have a faithful clientele. The prestige factor won't hurt your career either. When you visit or research a salon, be sure to check that the staff works actively with the clients by performing consultations, attending to their needs during the salon service, and not leaving them alone for too long while the service is processing. Basically, when researching a salon for job potential look for all of things you would want as a client. Just as you wouldn't want to get a manicure from a nail technician with poor hygiene, you wouldn't want to work in a salon where hygiene is not a priority.

Department Store Jobs

Department stores are always on the lookout for trained makeup artists, estheticians with makeup experience, and even hairdressers to work at their in-store salons. To learn more about what it's like to work in a particular store, do the following:

▶ **Mystery shop.** Go in as a customer. Quiz the people behind the counter on the different products and solicit their advice.
▶ **Talk to the employees.** Come in during a slow time (early morning or near closing is usually best) and ask them about what it's like to work there—what's expected of them, what the conditions are like, what the customers prefer, and so on. Ask for the name of a contact person to whom you can send your resume.
▶ **Send your resume and cover letter to the contact person or Human Resources office.** Follow up with a phone call a few days later.
▶ **Demonstrate your skills.** Offer to show the employer how great your skills are—your work will speak for itself.
▶ **Pull together a photo shoot so you can start a portfolio.** If you don't already know someone who is a photographer, ask around—your network is often your best resource!

Hiring is generally handled by the store's human resources office. Call to find out if it is accepting applications and what, if anything, you need to bring with you when you fill out your application. Aside from hair dressing and nail services, licenses are generally not required for these positions—but they never hurt.

Hotels

Hotels are another option for hair stylists—as well as for other beauty professionals such as massage therapists, nail technicians, and estheticians. Again, it's best to check out in person any place you think you might want to work. Book yourself an appointment and soak up the ambiance. If you think you'd like to work there, ask for the name of the person to whom you

How to Land Your First Job

should send a resume, and don't forget to follow up with a phone call. Also, it never hurts to ask the salon owner or manager if you can demonstrate your skills for them.

Cruise Ships

Do you dream of travel? Maybe a career on a cruise ship is for you. Most cruise ships have an onboard salon or spa and all of them need qualified professionals. Professionals are hired on a contract basis for a predetermined time period. Steiner Leisure operates spas on over 100 cruise ships. They offer contracts for four-month and eight-month periods. They hire hairdressers and stylists, nail technicians, massage therapists, estheticians, electrologists, and others to work in the onboard spas.

Many cruise ship operators have websites or toll-free phone numbers where you will be able to find out more information about job opportunities.

All Aboard

Cruise work can be fun and you can make good money take a look at this sample of jobs offered through www.cruiseshipjob.com:

▶ **Salon Manager** (oversees entire operations of the beauty salon, accounting and management of the salon staff): extensive beauty salon and managerial experience required. Salary range: $2,400-3,800 per month, depending on cruise lines.

▶ **Assistant Salon Manager** (manages the day-to-day operations of the beauty salon as directed by the salon manager): beauty salon and managerial experience required. Salary range: $2,000-2,900 per month, depending on cruise lines. Possibilities for promotion to Salon Manager.

▶ **Beauticians/Hair Stylists**: extensive beauty salon experience required. Fluent English language skills required. Salary range: $2,100-2,300 per month, depending on gratuities and cruise line. Possibilities for promotion to Assistant Salon Manager.

▶ **Massage Therapist**: extensive experience required. Good English language skills required. Salary range: $2,600-3,600 per month, depending on gratuities and cruise line.

91

FINDING YOUR JOB

You understand the importance of planning and you've given some thought to what you want out of a career. You've also started to research some of the physical places in which you could imagine yourself working. Now the question is, just how do you go about finding your first job? Luckily, there are many resources available for the job hunter, and a wise cosmetologist-to-be will take advantage of all of them. Keep in mind that most people apply for many jobs before they are accepted. Don't get discouraged if you send out a dozen resumes and hear from only two salons. That's just part of the process.

JUST THE FACTS

The cosmetology industry has plenty of entry-level jobs. In fact, thousands of them go unfilled each year, so finding openings shouldn't be difficult. Many of the entry-level jobs that were filled went to people with little experience. In fact, the NACCAS's 1999 Job Demand Survey reported that there were over 100,000 jobs in the industry that were filled by people with less than one year of experience.

JOB SEARCH RESOURCES

Your Cosmetology School

A great many reputable salons have forged relationships with excellent schools. Check the school's bulletin boards and work with their placement office to get an idea of local job possibilities. Also, visit the career office and get some tips on everything from creating a portfolio to writing a great resume.

Classified Advertising

Classified ads are an easy and inexpensive way to job hunt, and trade publications and your local newspaper are the two most reliable resources. Most trades come out monthly, but newspapers carry classified job advertising every day. If an entry catches your eye, apply immediately. If you're looking to move, check out the out-of-town newspapers at your local library, at large bookstores such as Barnes & Noble, or at the newspaper's website. One way to find out-of-town newspaper websites is to visit www.about.com and search for the area where you want to move. If the local newspaper has a website, it generally will be listed on the area's About.com site.

When you use the classified ads as a resource, look in the entry-level section for job titles in which you are interested. Your paper may have beauty or salon sections so you should look there as well. As with the out-of-town newspapers, you may be able to search your local classified ads online by visiting the website of your daily newspaper.

Nail Technicians in Demand

Of all the cosmetology specialties, nail technicians are in the highest demand. According to the most current information available, they make up less than 3% of the industry employees and yet they constitute 21% of all industry openings.

Source: "Job Demand in the Cosmetology Industry, 1999," a national survey conducted for the National Accrediting Commission of Cosmetology Arts and Sciences (NACCAS).

Career-Related Websites

On the Internet, there are literally thousands of career-related websites. Some of these sites offer how-to advice about landing a job. Others offer a database of job listings that can be searched by region, industry, job type, salary, position, job title, or almost any other criteria. There are also resume databases allowing applicants to post their resume in hopes of it getting read by a recruiter. If you need assistance creating your resume, there are professional resume writers who you can hire directly off the Web, many of whom also have informative websites of interest to job seekers.

The Internet is an extremely powerful job search tool that can not only help you find exciting job opportunities, but you can also research companies, network with other people in your field, and obtain valuable career-related advice. Using any Internet search engine or portal, you can enter a keyword such as: "resume," "job," "career," "job listings," or "help wanted" to find thousands of websites of interest to you. You can also use a keyword search that describes the type of job you're looking to fill, such as "hair stylist" or "nail technician." The following is a listing of just some of the general and beauty industry-specific online resources available to you:

ABA Resume Writing—www.abastaff.com/career/resume/resume.htm

About.com—jobsearch.about.com/jobs/jobsearch/msubrespost.htm

Accent Resume Writing—www.accent-resume-writing.com/critiques

Advanced Career Systems—www.resumesystems.com/career/Default.htm

America's Job Bank—www.ajb.dni.us

Behind the Chair—www.behindthechair.com

Best Jobs USA—www.bestjobsusa.com

Career Builder—www.careerbuilder.com

Career Center—www.jobweb.org/catapult/guenov/res.html#explore

Career Express—www.careerxpress.com

Career Spectrum—www.careerspectrum.com/dir-resume.htm

CareerMosaic—www.careermosaic.com

CareerNet—www.careers.org

CareerPath—www.careerpath.com

CareerWeb—www.cweb.com

Day Spa Association—www.dayspaassociation.com/employment/
    employment.htm

Day Spa Magazine Online—www.dayspamag.com

Hot Jobs—www.hotjobs.com

JobBank USA—www.jobbankusa.com

JobSource—www.jobsource.com

Nails Magazine Online—www.nailsmag.com

Occupational Outlook Handbook—stats.bls.gov/oco/oco1000.htm

(1)roof Community—www2.oneroof.org/interactive

Proven Resumes—www.free-resume-tips.com

Resumania—www.resumania.com

Salary.com—www.salary.com

Salon Force—www.salonforce.com

Salon Sense—www.salonsense.com/main.htm

Snip Magazine Online—www.snipmagazine.com

The Monster Board—www.monster.com

Yahoo Careers—careers.yahoo.com

Word of Mouth

Perhaps there is a salon in your metropolitan area for which you've always wanted to work, but you don't know what their hiring procedures are. First, dress for success. Bear in mind that first impressions, especially in this industry, really matter. You don't have to wear a suit, but you should be dressed neatly and professionally, with careful attention to hair, skin, and nails. Next, gather up your courage, go into the salon, and ask for an application. Another approach is to book a service and then chat with the hairdresser about the salon. Dress professionally and be polite and friendly with everyone. Ask some informative questions: How long has he or she been there? How did he or she get the job? What's it like to work there? Gauge your own feelings about the salon: Does it seem to be the kind of place you want to work? Would you be comfortable here? If you're still interested, talk to the person at the front desk about job openings, and take it from there.

Networking

Though networking is important, try not to think of it as a chore that comes with your job search. Networking just means getting to know people in the beauty industry and maintaining contact with them. This is a very positive and ongoing practice, and often getting together with other people in your profession won't seem like work. Networking relationships can provide many benefits:

▶ Mentoring
▶ Contacts within a prospective employment company
▶ Information about emerging technology
▶ Information about trends in the industry
▶ Cutting-edge training opportunities

Through networking, you may discover an opening in the hidden job market—meaning jobs that are never advertised. These jobs can account for up to 70–80% of all job vacancies. This market exists simply because of the large number of employers who are able to fill positions through word of mouth. Employers often feel that when they hire an employee who comes with a personal recommendation, it is like getting a guarantee. Use this to your advantage.

A good place to start networking is in beauty school. Many cosmetology instructors work in salons part-time and can be a great source of referrals for qualified student graduates. Also, consider asking your family and friends to introduce you to people they know who work in the beauty industry, especially if they have experience you can learn from or if they work in your area of interest. Last, don't discount your peers—consider peers who are energetic, personally motivated, and advancing in their field as good contacts, too.

EXPANDING YOUR CONTACT LIST

If a salon owner speaks to one of your classes or you take a seminar from a hair color specialist, ask for his or her business card. Ask the person a few questions, and then follow up the next day with a phone call or e-mail, to thank them or ask an additional question.

Also, consider requesting informational interviews at salons in your area. An informational interview is an excellent opportunity for you to learn more about how salons really work, gain interview experience, impress a contact who may be able to help you in the future, and better understand what people expect from their employees.

Remember that your contacts' willingness to help you will depend on how you ask. Keep your requests for help brief, conversational, and low-key. Above all, be sincere.

MAINTAINING YOUR CONTACTS

It is important to maintain contacts once you have established them. Try to contact people within two weeks of meeting them. You can ask a question, send a note of thanks, or a piece of information related to your conversation with them. This contact cements your meeting in their minds; they will remember you more readily when you contact them again. If you haven't been in contact with someone for a few months, you might send a note or e-mail about a relevant article you read. For example, if you read an article about a hot trend in hair coloring, you might want to photocopy it and send it to any hair color specialists you have met. This shows your contacts that you are truly interested in the industry and it keeps your name fresh in their minds. If they hear of a salon with an opening for someone who is responsible and enthusiastic, they'll think of you.

ORGANIZING YOUR CONTACT LIST

You can maintain your contact list in your planner—whether it is a handheld electronic planner or a traditional bound paper planner. Try to maintain the following pieces of information about each person:

- ▶ name
- ▶ address
- ▶ e-mail address
- ▶ phone number(s)
- ▶ fax number
- ▶ company
- ▶ position/specialty (salon owner, electrologist, instructor)
- ▶ first meeting (where, when, what topics did you discuss?)
- ▶ last contact (when, why, and how)

YOUR STATE COSMETOLOGY ASSOCIATION

Some state cosmetology associations carry job listings as a matter of course. Use the list in Appendix A to find your state cosmetology association. This is an excellent resource if you are looking to relocate. By visiting your state cosmetology association website, you will also learn of new legislation effecting cosmetologists and other news that may impact your career.

Now that you know where the jobs are and how to find the best ones, and you have the training to fill one or more of the openings you find, the next step in the process is to create your resume and cover letter, then start actually applying for the jobs that are of interest. The next chapter will walk you through the resume, cover letter, and portfolio creation process. You also will learn how to prepare for your interviews and put your best face forward to really impress potential employers.

THE INSIDE TRACK

Who:	Brian Fallon
What:	Manager, Educational Programming
Where:	Pivot Point International, Inc.
	Chicago, Illinois

I have always been fascinated by the way people express themselves through the way they look, their physicality. I wanted to have a part in helping individuals create that form of expression for themselves. And beauty, in all forms, is of great importance to me.

I went through basic cosmetology and teacher training, a total of about 2,500 hours. Prior to being trained as a cosmetologist, however, I studied Fine Arts. My background in portraiture and fashion illustration has been absolutely invaluable to me in this profession. I am able to communicate ideas, such as bridal designs, easily and without a lot of words. This leaves less room for misunderstanding.

I work 45-55 hours each week for an educational company, producing educational materials for the cosmetology industry. I've worked for the same company for 14 years now, with a number of incredibly talented cosmetologists. I have had the opportunity to travel extensively, working on a variety of educational projects over the years. I have been exposed to the editorial end of our business also, through my participation in countless photo shoots.

I am not in a salon full-time, and never have been. I have worked in a number of salons on a part-time basis while working for my current employer. As a hairstylist, I specialize in long hair design. I am also proficient with makeup design. However, being behind a chair full-time never appealed to me. I like the variety that my job offers me.

I've also done a great deal of work for weddings. In addition to designing hair for the bride, I design and create custom headpieces and veils. I also offer to chop for headpieces or veils if the client would rather go that route. I am usually available to view the actual gown as it is being decided upon, allowing me to offer input. I try to be available during pre-ceremony photo shoots as well. As a rule, I do hair only for the bride, and prefer to have the bridal party and other family done by another hair designer. This allows me to focus on the bride, without any pressure on myself to hurry and fit others in. I find that it also helps to keep the bride more focused and calm as the preparations proceed.

The biggest challenge I have faced is dealing with the stereotypes that exist around the profession. In my opinion, this stereotyping, with the assumption that hairdressers are intellectually inferior, is done as much by hairdressers as by those outside the industry. In reality, there are many wonderful and challenging opportunities to express oneself creatively in this field—and many talented people to work with and look up to.

CHAPTER five

RESUMES, COVER LETTERS, AND INTERVIEWS

PREPARING A resume. Writing a cover letter. Promoting yourself in an interview. These tasks can produce some serious anxiety. This chapter aims to reduce that anxiety by outlining the steps you will need to take to put together a solid resume, craft a professional cover letter, and present a polished and qualified image at your interviews. You will also learn how to develop your portfolio and gain some inside information on what employers look for during interviews.

RESUME AND COVER LETTER BASICS

Once you have identified the job opportunities you plan to pursue, you will need to use a resume, cover letter, and possibly a portfolio of your work to apply for those jobs. Combined, these are an extremely important tool for securing interviews and, ultimately, a job. Be sure you take whatever time is necessary to create well-written documents that clearly represent who you are and what qualifications you have. Unless you already have met them, potential employers will develop their first impressions of you based on your cover letter and resume.

An absolute must for both your resume and your cover letter: Make sure you proofread them for errors in spelling, grammar, and sense before you mail them out. A typo can happen to anyone, but savvy salon owners will take note of it, and while they won't necessarily think you're unintelligent, they will think you don't take the time to check your work, and they may question your thoroughness. Don't give them the opportunity. Always read your resume and cover letter twice; if possible, ask a friend or a colleague to read them, too. A fresh pair of eyes is more likely to catch a mistake.

THE RESUME

A resume is a one-page summary of your qualifications, experience, and interests that you will send to prospective employers. This summary can act as your introduction by mail, or as your calling card if you are applying for a position in person. You don't need to tailor it for each position you apply to, however. That's what a cover letter—a brief note of introduction explaining who you are and why you are interested in a particular position—is for.

Highlights

Your resume is meant to capture the interest of potential employers, so they will call you for a personal interview. That means your resume should highlight your:

▶ Career objective(s)

▶ Education

▶ Employment history and related experience

▶ Special skills and/or personal qualifications

The importance of a resume should not be underestimated. It is essential to landing a job in any salon, whether you are a new graduate or an experienced, licensed professional. The bottom line: A resume proves to potential employers that you are serious about your career as a cosmetologist and as a professional.

In fact, some salon owners will not interview candidates who don't have resumes. The top salons and spas want to hire cosmetologists who are proud of their accomplishments and who view themselves as professionals. A cosmetology resume shows just that. However, your resume shouldn't simply list your cosmetology school and course work. You want your resume to stand out so you should include information that will help it to do that. If you have ever interned at a salon, assisted a hairstylist, nail technician, or esthetician, or had experience with hair color, include that on your resume. You should also list all trade shows, additional educational classes, and beauty conventions that you have attended, as well as all other non-related work experience to prove your stability, initiative, and career commitment. For example, hair color skills are in high demand in most salons across the country, so any experience or course work in this area will be viewed as a bonus and should be listed on your resume.

What Should You Include?

Resumes should state the facts, in as brief and concise a manner as possible. Here is what's relevant:

▶ Your professional experience (not just in a salon—any work experience that shows you are capable and responsible). Supply your job titles, one- or two-sentence descriptions of what you did, and the dates for each job.
▶ Your education
▶ Special skills, awards, and citations
▶ Any other work or interests you feel are pertinent

Do **not** include:

▶ Your marital status
▶ Your age, race, or religion
▶ Personal interests that have no bearing on the job
▶ Reasons for leaving previous jobs

It is very important that you are honest about your accomplishments on your resume. Some people mistakenly think that because they do not have much experience, they should stretch the truth to make them more appealing to potential employers. Don't make this mistake. Employers have a variety of ways to check that the information you provide on your resume is accurate, so if you lie, you may get caught. You may be a whiz with highlights, but if you aren't honest that hip salon won't want to hire you. So be positive about your accomplishments, just keep it truthful.

Putting It On Paper

Start by putting your name, address, and telephone number(s) at the top of your resume. If you have an e-mail address, include that, too.

Objective

Under your name and address, you will need to state your job objective, which is your reason for contacting the employer. Under the heading *Objective*, describe briefly what you hope to accomplish in your job search, such as "To obtain an entry-level position in esthetics at a skincare or full-service beauty salon."

Education/Training

List the schools you have attended in reverse chronological order, starting with your most recent training, and ending with the least recent. Employers want to be able to see your highest qualifications first. For each educational experience, include dates attended, name and location of school, and degree or certificate earned. If you have not attended college, end with your high school; if you have attended college, it is not necessary to list your high school unless you attended a vocational program, or you took cosmetology courses while in high school.

If you have attended any beauty seminars that were not part of your training program, you should list them here. For example, if you recently attended a daylong workshop on Acrylic Alternatives, you would list the name of the seminar, the organization that ran it, and the dated you attended.

Work Experience

If you don't have much to list in this section, don't panic. It is not uncommon for recent cosmetology school graduates to have limited work experience. If you do have related work experience, list it in reverse chronological order, just like you listed your education/training. Include company name and location (city, state), the position you held, and the date of employment. Write a few lines describing the nature of your work.

What if you don't have any related experience yet? List any employment experiences you've had where you've developed the skills and traits needed to become a successful cosmetologist. Your potential employer is looking to hire someone who can work well in a team environment, is responsible, will present a positive, fashionable image to clients, and who can move from task to task easily. If you had a part-time job while you were in cosmetology school, list it, even if it seems completely unrelated to the beauty industry. Your ability to hold a job while in school will show potential employers that you can manage you time effectively.

Special Skills

You may wish to include another section called *Special Skills*, *Awards*, or *Personal Qualifications*. When you do not yet have a lot of experience, this is a section that can help you stand apart from the crowd. Items that you may want to include in this section are:

▶ Awards won during your training program
▶ Languages (in addition to English) that you speak
▶ Special certifications not directly related to cosmetology such as CPR (many service businesses look to have someone with first aid skills on their staff)

Sample resumes are shown at the end of this chapter.

THE COVER LETTER

Cover letters should be a little more personal than a resume, but always professional. Make specific reference to the position you desire, and briefly express why you'd be the best candidate for it. Your letter should not be too long (no more than one page); nor should it sound like a sales pitch. Think of it as a letter of introduction, in which you want to show that you're both mature and interesting.

If you are applying to a position based on the recommendation or referral of a contact, it is important to mention that in your letter. Be sure to check with your contact first. Once you have secured permission to mention your contact by name, your resume will likely stand out from the rest and help you get noticed.

Sample cover letters are shown at the end of this chapter.

GATHERING INFORMATION

Now that you understand what should and should not be included in your resume and cover letter, you need to gather all of the critical information necessary to produce the resume and letter. Sure, you know where you went to school, but can you concisely describe the top four skills you developed there? The following questionnaire will help you to collect the information that will be useful not only for your resume and cover letter but later for your interview as well.

Personal Skills

What do you believe is your most marketable skill? Why?

_____

_____

_____

_____

List three or four specific examples of how you have used this skill either at work or in your training program. What was accomplished as a result?

1. _____
2. _____
3. _____
4. _____

What is another of your marketable skills? _____

Provide at least three examples of how you've used this skill:

1. _____
2. _____
3. _____

What unusual or unique skill(s) do you possess that help you stand out from other applicants applying for the same types of positions as you?

_____

_____

What skills do you believe you currently lack?

_____

_____

What skills do you have, but that need to be polished or enhanced in order to make you a more appealing candidate?

_____

_____

Writing out your most marketable personal skills will especially help you to know what to highlight in your cover letter.

Work/Employment History

Most recent employer: _____

City, State: _____

Year you began work: _____

Year you stopped working (write "Present" if still employed): _____

Job title: _____

Job description: _____

_____

_____

Reason for leaving: _____

_____

What was your biggest accomplishment while holding this job? _____

_____

_____

Contact person at the company who can provide a reference: _____

Contact person's phone number: _____

Annual salary/Wage per hour: _____

Employer: _____

City, State: _____

Year you began work: _____

Year you stopped working (write "Present" if still employed): _____

Job title: _____

Job description: _____

_____

_____

Reason for leaving:_____

What was your biggest accomplishment while holding this job?_____

_____

_____

Contact person at the company who can provide a reference:_____

Contact person's phone number:_____

Annual salary/Wage per hour:_____

Complete these employment-related questions for all of your previous employers, including part-time, temporary and summer jobs, and apprenticeships.

When you communicate with potential employers, however, you won't want to reveal your past earning history upfront. You will want this information available to you as reference, however, when you begin negotiating your future salary, benefits, and overall compensation package.

Military Service (if applicable)

Branch of service you served in:_____

Years served:_____

Highest rank achieved:_____

Decorations or awards earned:_____

Special skills or training you obtained:_____

_____

Professional Accreditations & Licenses_____

_____

List all of the professional accreditations and/or licenses you have earned thus far. If you are taking the state cosmetology licensing exam at a date in the future, enter that information here._____

_____

Hobbies & Special Interests

List any hobbies or special interests you have that are not necessarily work-related, but that potentially could be adapted for the workplace, setting you apart from the competition (for example, computer skills that could translate to the ability to help a salon owner create a better website): _____

_____

_____

_____

What non-professional clubs or organizations do you belong to or actively participate in? _____

_____

Personal/Professional Ambitions

What are your long-term goals? _____

_____

Personal: _____

_____

Professional: _____

_____

Financial: _____

_____

_____

For your personal, professional and financial goals, what are three smaller, short-term goals you can begin working toward achieving right now that will help you ultimately achieve each of your long-term goals?

Short-Term Personal Goals
1. _____
2. _____
3. _____

Short-Term Professional Goals
1. _____
2. _____
3. _____

Short-Term Financial Goals

1. _____

2. _____

3. _____

Will the job(s) you will be applying for help you achieve your long-term goals and objectives? If *yes*, how? If *no*, why not? _____

_____

_____

_____

What would you most like to improve about your life overall? _____

_____

_____

_____

What are a few things you can do, starting immediately, to bring about positive changes in your personal, professional, or financial life? _____

_____

_____

_____

Where would you like to be personally, professionally, and financially five years from now? _____

_____

_____

_____

What needs to be done to achieve these long-term goals or objectives? _____

_____

_____

_____

What are some of the qualities about yourself, your appearance, and your personality that you're most proud of? _____

_____

_____

_____

What are some of the qualities about yourself, your appearance, and your personality that you believe need improvement? _____

_____

_____

_____

What do others most like about you? _____

_____

_____

_____

What do you think others least like about you? _____

_____

_____

_____

If you decided to pursue additional education, what would you study and why? How would this help you professionally? _____

_____

_____

_____

If you had more free time, what would you spend it doing? _____

_____

_____

_____

List several accomplishments in your personal and professional life that you're most proud of. Why did you choose these things?

1. _____
2. _____
3. _____
4. _____
5. _____

What do you believe is your biggest weakness? Why wouldn't an employer hire you? _____

_____

_____

_____

What would be the ideal atmosphere for you to work in? Would you prefer a large day spa, small salon, or busy department store salon? _____

_____

_____

_____

List three qualities about a new job that would make it the ideal employment opportunity for you:

1. _____

2. _____

3. _____

What type of coworkers would you prefer to have? _____

_____

_____

_____

When it comes to work-related benefits and perks, what's most important to you? _____

_____

_____

_____

When you're recognized for doing a good job at work, how do you like to be rewarded? _____

_____

_____

_____

If you were to write a help wanted ad describing your dream job, what would the ad say? _____

_____

_____

_____

You should be able to begin building your resume from the information collected in this questionnaire. For resume wording and formatting, follow the guidelines in this book or purchase one that specifically contains sample resumes from which you can obtain ideas. However you create your resume, never copy it right out of a book. Employers will notice, and it won't reflect the real you. You can use the sample resumes provided here or in other books as a guide, but the content should be 100% accurate and customized to you.

SAMPLE RESUME 1

Emily Prescott
1230 Hillside Ave.
Schenectady, NY 12305
518-555-0101

Objective: An assistant-level position at a high-quality salon that will provide me with the experience and skills necessary to become a haircolor specialist.

Professional Experience
Assistant Manager, Books and Such, Schenectady, NY
June 1997–August 1999
Responsible for store operations during scheduled shifts; supervised staff, handled in-store promotions. Dealt with customer-service issues.

Educational Experience
Orlo Beauty School, Albany, NY, Graduated May 2001.
Course work included haircutting (theory and technique), permanent waving, relaxing, multicultural hair (including locking and hair extensions), wigs, and hairpieces. Finished a mini-curriculum in haircolor.

Schenectady County Community College, 1997–1998
Took courses in accounting, bookkeeping, and small-business management.

Other Skills
- Knowledge of Microsoft applications including Excel, Word and Access
- Conversant in Spanish

References furnished upon request.

COVER LETTER 1

Emily Prescott
1230 Hillside Ave.
Schenectady, NY 12305
September 25, 2001

Abbie O'Connor
Hair Flair
1313 Central Avenue
Albany, NY 12203

Dear Ms. O'Connor,

I am writing in response to your advertisement in the Sunday's *Times Union*, in which you announced an opening for a hair-dresser's assistant at Hair Flair.

As the enclosed copy of my resume indicates, my experience is extensive and varied. I recently graduated from the Orlo Beauty School in Albany and received my state cosmetology license. During my education, I won numerous awards, including "Most Dedicated" in my class. Prior to beauty school, I was an assistant manager at Books and Such, an independent bookstore located in Schenectady. In this position, I gained experience setting goals and completing projects in a timely and thorough manner as well as developing my customer service and client relationship skills.

I would like to meet with you and will contact your office the week of October 1 to determine if an interview may be arranged. If you wish to contact me before that date, please call 555-0101.

Sincerely,

Emily Prescott
Emily Prescott
Enc.

SAMPLE RESUME 2

Caroline Matusic
15 Dovetail Lane
Columbus, OH 43215
614-555-7777

Objective
To obtain an entry-level position at a full-service beauty salon.

Education
Austin Beauty Academy, Columbus, OH
Graduated December 2001

Westmont High School, Westmont, OH
Graduated June 1999, with honors

Professional Experience
Medical Receptionist Riverview Medical Center, Columbus, OH
June 1999–present
- Worked part-time while attending beauty school
- Answered phones, scheduled appointments, greeted patients

Waitress, TGI Fridays, Columbus, OH
September 1998–December 1999
- Worked part-time while attending high-school and after graduation

Other Qualifications
- Organized a day of beauty for residents of a local women's shelter at the Austin Beauty Academy.
- "Best Touch" award for December 2001 graduating class at Austin Beauty Academy.

References available upon request.

SAMPLE COVER LETTER 2

Caroline Matusic
15 Dovetail Lane
Columbus, OH 43215
December 15, 2001

Jean-Paul Roberge
The Jean-Paul Salon
515 North Park Street
Columbus, OH 43320

Dear Mr. Roberge,

Your ad in the *Daily News* for an assistant position at The Jean-Paul Salon caught my attention, as I am preparing to begin my professional career. I just completed my training program at the Austin Beauty Academy. I will be taking the state boards later this month and feel confident that my education has prepared me well to pass with ease.

As you will see on the enclosed resume, I supplemented my cosmetology training with a part-time position as a receptionist at the Riverview Medical Center. I am experienced in handling general office duties and answering phones cordially and courteously. I believe that these skills can be as useful in a salon environment as they are in a doctor's office.

I am a reliable, detail-oriented, and extremely hard-working person with a strong desire to have a successful career as a hair stylist. Your salon has an excellent reputation throughout Columbus and I hope that I am able to develop my skills and learn how to be a top-rate stylist from you.

I would welcome the chance to discuss the assistant position you currently have open. If you will contact me at 614-555-7777, we can schedule a meeting.

Thank you for your consideration.

Sincerely,

Caroline Matusic

Caroline Matusic
Enclosure.

THE INTERVIEW

If your cover letter and resume catch a prospective employer's eye, then it is likely you will be contacted for a personal interview. The interview gives the employer a chance to size you up, and it gives you the chance to learn more about the position and, if appropriate, make a more detailed case for yourself as the best candidate for the job.

Job interviews are important because first impressions are critical—particularly in the beauty industry, where your appearance can mean the difference between being fully booked and spending your time cleaning the supply closet.

Preparing for Your Interview

Try to set your first interview for at least one week in the future. Though you are anxious to start your new career, you want to be sure that you have enough time to be fully prepared. Giving yourself a week to prepare will ensure that you have the confidence you need to make a good impression. Here is a list of preparation steps to follow for a successful interview.

Know Where You Are Going

Once the interview is set, make sure you know exactly where it will occur. If you are interviewing at a franchise in a shopping mall, for instance, you want to be sure that you are going to the right mall—many cities have several malls, some of which have the same retail stores and services. If you are interviewing at an unfamiliar salon, get directions. It is a good idea to drive to the location once before your interview. This way, you will have a better idea of how long it will take you to get to the interview, and leave yourself extra time for driving or commuting, especially during rush hour. Being late for an interview is like having a typo on your resume. You never get another chance to make a first impression.

Practice

Enlist someone to ask you tough questions and then give you feedback on your answers. Or, stand in front of a mirror and practice your responses to possible questions. Practicing will increase your confidence and that will increase your likelihood of landing the job. Read on to see the sample questions on page 121.

Exercise

Go for a walk, a run, take a class like step, yoga, or Pilates. The point here is that very few things release stress the way exercise does. So take the time to treat your body right. The boost you get from exercise will help you to be more alert and creative during your interview.

Get a Good Night's Sleep

Who needs dark circles under their eyes the day of an interview? Stick to your regular sleep schedule the week before your interview and try to get a solid eight hours the night before.

Eat

This is simple. It is impossible to perform at your best on an empty stomach, or one that has been fed with low-quality food. Eat light but filling fare the day of the interview, and stick with foods that are common in your diet. That hot new Malaysian restaurant may be tempting but if you've never had Malaysian food, do you really want to try it two hours before an important interview? That's best left for a celebratory meal after you've landed the job.

Get Your Materials in Order

You should bring at least one copy of your resume to your interview, even if the company already has it, and a list of questions to ask your interviewer. If you take the time to prepare a list of questions, your potential employer will view you as responsible and dedicated. Write out at least five questions to ask and read them over a few times before your interview. You might want to create a personal sheet of notes that outlines your strengths and special skills. Having such a sheet handy will help you remember things when you feel on the spot and your memory may not be what it should be. Relying on it will also help you to remain confident throughout the interview.

Plan Your Outfit

Don't wait for the last minute to decide what you will wear on your interview. Once you have your interview scheduled, plan an outfit that fits well and is clean and pressed. If an outfit needs to be dry-cleaned, take it to the cleaners so that you can get it back at least three days before your interview. Nothing is worse than planning to wear something, picking it up at the cleaners the day of your interview and finding out the outfit shrunk or was in some other way ruined. If you have given yourself plenty of time and the worst happens, you will be able to put together a new outfit.

The biggest turn-off to salon owners is when job candidates dress as if they are running their daily errands or as if they don't care about the job they are interviewing for. A nice business suit, dress, or pantsuit is suitable; your hairstyle and makeup should be impeccable to reflect your dedication to image. Your outfit should be fashionable but not over-the-top trendy. (A sassy handbag in the most au courant style is great, but head-to-toe fashion fad is not.) Most salon owners will expect you to keep up this image at work after you are hired.

Allow Sufficient Time for the Interview

Often, interviews are set up so that you will meet with more than one person during the interview cycle, adding time to the length of the interview. You will not be at your best if you are worried about another appointment. It is a mistake to rush your interviewers because you have made a previous and conflicting commitment for the same day.

Arrive Early

Arriving at your interview early shows that you are professional and that you respect your interviewer and his or her time. You should attempt to arrive at the interview approximately ten minutes before the scheduled time. While you want to be early, you do not want to be too early. If you arrive substantially early, wait to enter the location so that you are arriving only ten minutes early. Allow extra travel time if you are unfamiliar with the employer's location to accommodate any delays.

JUST THE FACTS

Communication and people skills are very important for a cosmetologist. A hairstylist or nail technician may have the best technical skills possible, but if they don't also have excellent communication or people skills, many salon owners will not hire them.

AT THE INTERVIEW

You've done your homework and are well-prepared. You look great. Now, it is time to impress your potential employer. Start off by keeping a positive frame of mind. If your interview begins on a down beat, it may be difficult to turn the atmosphere around into a positive situation later. Remember to turn any negatives into positives right away. Be sure that you are projecting a positive attitude by remembering to smile and keep eye contact with your interviewer.

In addition to a traditional interview, some salons incorporate staff inter-action into the process. This involves a day when the applicant comes in for three to four hours to observe and interact with staff. During the day, the applicant meets the staff and is often encouraged to spend time with each staff member to get to know a little bit about them. This includes current assistants, hair designers, receptionists, estheticians, and nail technicians. The benefit of this type of interview is that you can observe each professional at work, and can study their technique not only in cutting and styling, but also how they interact with their clients. If you are invited to this type of interview, be sure you ask the stylists lots of questions to learn about how the salon really works.

Take the Time to Listen

Don't be so intent on selling yourself that you seem overeager. Avoid interrupting your interviewer and don't just repeat what has been said. Take your time in replying to questions. A slow, thoughtful response is best. Smile—and breathe. Remember: A salon professional is called upon to listen far more than he or she is called upon to talk. Show the interviewer that you have what it takes to be a confidante, not a performer.

Interview Questions

After introductions, your interviewer will ask you a number of questions. The exact nature will depend on the position and the interviewer's personal style. Below are some interview questions frequently asked by employers. Think about how you would answer as you read through the list. Practice these answers well before you are on your way to the interview.

- ▶ Why should we hire you?
- ▶ What are your career objectives?
- ▶ Tell me a little about yourself.
- ▶ Tell me about your training program.
- ▶ If you could have the perfect position, what would it be?
- ▶ Why did you choose cosmetology?
- ▶ In what type of position are you most interested?
- ▶ What do you expect to be doing in five years?
- ▶ What is your previous work experience? What have you gained or learned from it?
- ▶ Why are you interested in our salon and in this particular opening?
- ▶ What do you consider to be your major strengths and weaknesses?
- ▶ In what ways do you think you can make a contribution to our service?
- ▶ What two or three accomplishments have given you the most satisfaction?
- ▶ What have you done to show initiative and willingness to work?
- ▶ Do you subscribe to trade journals or magazines? If so, which ones?
- ▶ What jobs have you enjoyed the most? The least? Why?
- ▶ What qualifications do you have that make you feel you will be successful in this field?

Interviewing the Salon

An interview works two ways: The salon owner wants to find out about you, and you should be prepared to interview the salon. Frequently, toward the close of the interview, the interviewer will provide you with the opportunity to ask questions. Don't ever say that you don't have any questions. This is your chance to set yourself apart from the competition. Prepare your questions in advance, and ask the most important questions first, in case there is not enough time to ask all of them. Do not ask questions that might show a lack of research.

Educational Questions

Ask about future potential opportunities for career education. Showing an interest in education shows an interest in your career and its future.

- ▶ Will the salon owner provide educational seminars?
- ▶ Will there be opportunities for hands-on training?
- ▶ How often are educational seminars conducted?
- ▶ Who will pay for them?
- ▶ What other help can you offer as I move up and become more experienced?

Salon Questions

Ask everyone you meet about the salon.

- ▶ How long have they worked there?
- ▶ Did they go through a training program?
- ▶ How many clients per month does the salon service?
- ▶ Where do new clients come from and how are they distributed?
- ▶ How many of the current staff members were assistants?
- ▶ What brands of professional products does the salon carry?
- ▶ How many clients does each salon professional typical have?
- ▶ What makes the salon unique in its market?
- ▶ What are this salon's plans for future growth?
- ▶ What is the rate of turnover at the salon?
- ▶ What is the salon's marketing strategy?
- ▶ What are the salon's strengths and weaknesses?
- ▶ Who is the typical client?
- ▶ How would you describe the other stylists?

Employment Questions

Don't be afraid to ask about how you will be compensated, but don't sound overly concerned about money.

- ▶ Is the salon commission or salary based?
- ▶ Are health benefits offered?
- ▶ How much can I expect to make as an assistant?
- ▶ How will my compensation package change when I become a hairstylist?
- ▶ Is there a 401(k) or some other form of employee savings plan?
- ▶ How often will I be paid?
- ▶ Is there a training or procedures manual in which my specific duties or responsibilities are spelled out?
- ▶ What do you do to market, advertise, and publicize the salon?
- ▶ What types of promotions, events, and charitable programs do you sponsor?

Follow-Up Strategy

Send a courtesy letter to thank the interviewer for the opportunity to speak with her or him. Mention the time and date of the original interview and any important points discussed. Include important qualifications that you may have omitted in the interview, and reiterate your interest in the job.

Do not be discouraged if a definite offer is not made at the interview, or if a specific salary is not discussed. The interviewer will usually communicate with her or his office staff or interview other applicants before making an offer. Generally, a decision is reached within a few weeks. Remember to keep track of interviews in your planner, and note the time period in which the interviewer says you will hear from her or him. If you do not hear from the salon within that amount of time, follow up with a telephone call. However, you must show a commitment to their timetable. Don't call too soon or more than once.

If you are like most other cosmetologists, you may not get the first job you apply for. If this is the case, return to the beginning of the process, and look for available positions. Take stock of why you may not have been offered a job, too. If the reason(s) had to do with your interview skills, lack of training, or some other correctable item, work on it before applying again. Once you do land a job, you will want to read Chapter 6 carefully for information about how to succeed.

Important Qualities

In addition to your resume, cover letter, and portfolio, once you meet with a potential employer he or she will be evaluating you on a number of intangible qualities. In many cases, these qualities are more important to an employer than an impressive resume. Some qualities that they look for include:

▶ Self-confidence without arrogance

▶ Self-motivation

▶ Image consciousness and pride in appearance

▶ Extroverted behavior

▶ Ability to listen

▶ Fashionable, definable sense of style

▶ Positive, upbeat, easy-going personality

Exuding these traits will show employers that you will thrive in a team environment, project an image that is in concert with the salon's and be able to get along with clients.

Compensation Issues

As they do in many service professions, cosmetology pay schemes vary widely and there are pros and cons to each method.

Salary or Hourly Wage
This method guarantees you a fixed income for the hours you work. It offers stability and means you are an employee of the salon. On the negative side, salaries themselves offer little incentive to increase productivity—you get paid the same, regardless of whether you work on two clients a day or ten.

Salary or Hourly Wage Plus Commission
This combines the security of a regular paycheck with a bonus for hitting certain targets—service dollars, retail dollars, or a combination thereof.

Commission Only

This offers you no security but a chance to make a very large sum indeed. It all depends, however, on the percentage at which your commission is set. If you do $500 worth of services a day and your commission is 50%, then you will receive $250 before taxes for the day's work. If there's a thunderstorm and no one leaves his or her house that day, you may not make a dime.

Sliding-Scale Commission

Higher-end salons that are sophisticated in the retailing arena often utilize this method. For instance, your commission may be 30% up to the first $1,000 you generate that week in service sales; then it may shoot up to 40% for the next $1,000, and to 50% for the next $1,000. Or you may make commission on retail products at a rate of, say, 20%, provided you sell a minimum of $500 worth of retail every week.

Renting or Leasing Space

This arrangement means you're an independent contractor with your own station in a salon with other independent contractors. You are not an employee of the salon, and therefore you are not eligible for benefits.

Think long and hard about the compensation program at the salon you'd like to work for before saying *yes* to any job offer. The reasons are multifaceted: If you're just starting out your career, you don't have a clientele yet—so a commission-only situation may be a tough go. Beginning salaries, although often low, are at least guaranteed income. Once you're more experienced and have established a roster of steady clients, a salary-plus-commission or commission-only situation becomes a little more realistic. And if you rent space, you will have to purchase all of your own equipment, and you will incur other expenses you might not have considered.

The Importance of Benefits

Be sure to ask your prospective employer about the salon's benefits program. Specifically, query them about the following items.

COSMETOLOGY career starter

Health Insurance

A workplace standard in other industries, health insurance is less common in salons. But over the last couple of years, more salon owners—and especially those who own more than one location—have committed to offering insurance to attract higher-quality employees.

Company-Funded Profit Sharing

Forward-thinking salons may offer some type of profit-sharing, to which both the employer and employee contribute. Employees become fully vested in the plan after a period of years.

401(k) Plans

As with profit-sharing, both parties kick in contributions to this plan. However, you can't withdraw the money before age $59\frac{1}{2}$ without a steep penalty, making this an ideal retirement account.

Paid Vacations

An obvious perk and while pretty low on the priority level, it is certainly one you will come to appreciate when you enter the work force.

Flex Time

Some salons will permit you, after you begin earning a certain amount of revenue, to alter your hours to suit your schedule. You may still work 40 hours, but not in the conventional five-day increments. This is becoming more commonplace as salons stay open later and even on Sunday to accommodate time-crunched clients.

Training Programs and Education

Ask whether the salon will foot the bill for any advanced classes or seminars you'd like to take, or whether the salon brings in educators on its own. Some salons will help you pay for a trip to an out-of-town trade show, with the understanding that you will share what you've learned with the rest of the staff upon your return.

ABOUT YOUR PORTFOLIO

A portfolio of your work is always impressive, although it may not be completely necessary when you are first starting out. To put one together, collect photographs of your finished work, whether it is hairstyles, hair color, makeup, nail care, or makeovers, to display in a professional-looking portfolio.

If you don't have photos of work you have done, get a friend or relative to act as a model. Snap before-and-after shots of them. As you continue on in your career, ask clients if you can photograph them so that you can add to your portfolio.

You now know the basics about the resume, cover letter, interview process, and portfolio. Get out there and get your job!

THE INSIDE TRACK

Who: Domenico Sereno
What: Owner, Daniela Hair Salon
Where: New York City

I learned how to cut hair as a teenager in the small village that I grew up in near Sorrento, in Italy. The economy in southern Italy in the 1960s wasn't very good, and everybody was poor—really poor. There weren't many options for a young man back then. My three older brothers moved to Germany or America to find work, because in my village, you could either be a fisherman, a policeman, a mason, a butcher, or a farmer—that was it. None of those options seemed very appealing to me. Like most young guys, when I dreamed about what I wanted to do with myself, I pictured traveling the world, meeting beautiful girls, and one day being rich. But Italy was not exactly the land of opportunity, and I was being pressured by my father to find a trade, or join him on the fishing boats.

So I guess I was about sixteen, and my older sister Philomena was getting married. Usually, our mother would cut our hair, but because this was a special occasion, I went to the town barber, Antonello. When he was cutting my hair, he asked me what I planned on doing with my life. I told him about my dreams, and I expected him to laugh at me.

But he didn't. He offered me a job as his apprentice—I would help him out around his shop, and he would teach me how to cut hair. He told me about the big salons in Rome and Milan, and about his friends in those cities who opened salons and became wealthy. He said if I worked hard and paid attention to him, when I was ready I could go out and find work anywhere. That sounded good to me, and that is exactly what I did.

I eventually made it to Milan and found work as a stylist at fashion shows when they were in season. That is where I met my wife, who is an American from New York. When I moved to New York, I made it a point to work as much as I could. Working hard is important for anybody who wants to be successful in this business—it builds your clientele, and the more you work, the more knowledgeable and skilled you become. I opened up my first shop when I thought I had a big enough base of customers to sustain my business. At first, I don't think I was really prepared for it. If you have never run a small business before, and you jump into it, it is very easy to find yourself in over your head. But somehow I managed, and eventually thrived. My customers are very loyal. I have done women's hair on their wedding day, and then been privileged to have done their daughter's hair on the same occasion 25 years later! Repeat customers are a must for any successful hairstylist, so it is important that you are good at what you do, and have a colorful personality while you are doing it.

When I hire stylists for my salon, there are a number of factors I look for in candidates. First off, I look for skill and professionalism—that is very important. But just as important as their styling skills are their people skills. You can be a wizard with the scissors, but if you have a bad attitude, that just doesn't cut it (pardon the pun!). A candidate should always make a point to look good—neat, clean, and professional. We are in the business of appearances, and if a stylist doesn't seem to be aware of fashion or good taste, that says a lot to a client. And of course, a stylist should always be on the cusp of the latest fashions. That means reading magazines, going to shows, keeping their eyes open! There are many stylists out there that are very good—you have to think how you can make yourself better. That is the key to success in any profession.

My advice to anyone interested in becoming a hairstylist is exactly what my mentor back in Italy said to me—work hard and pay attention. This business can be fun and rewarding for the right type of person. If you are artistic, fashion conscious, and love being around people, you'll quickly realize you've made the right choice. Good luck!

CHAPTER six

HOW TO SUCCEED ON THE JOB

YOUR FIRST job should be one that you will thoroughly enjoy and that will lead you toward future career advancement. The skills and habits you develop now are part of the foundation that will determine the level of success you enjoy in your career. Two important skills for you to develop are the ability to forge positive relationships with your boss and coworkers and to fit into the culture at your new salon. These skills go hand-in-hand. You will also learn about paying your dues and moving up, managing your time, finding a mentor, and making your mark while on the job.

YOU'VE FOUND what looks to be your dream job—at least your dream *first* job. However, it's not likely that you will be jumping in to work on clients right away. You may have to go through a training or trial period. During this time, you may feel a bit excluded from the action. The owner or manager may not have much time for you—she's got a business to run and at least 20 other employees vying for her attention. You may wonder if this is the career you really want?

Of course it is! You are just experiencing what every new cosmetology professional experiences. This is the sometimes rocky transition from school to salon. Entry-level jobs are often considered glorified apprenticeships, and you will have to spend plenty of time mixing haircolor formula and sweeping up hair before you can move up to having your own chair and clientele.

You will also have to learn how to handle a wide variety of personalities and work with them peacefully for 40 hours or more a week. While this may be frustrating in the beginning, the reward will come in the form of a challenging, successful, and enjoyable career.

Success Strategy

There are two things you don't want to be on your first day—overdressed or underdressed. Plan your first day outfit based on the types of outfits you saw stylists wearing during your interview.

STARTING OUT

As you start your career you need to keep in mind that there is only so much you can learn at a beauty school, even a top-notch one. You may feel thoroughly knowledgeable about the technical aspects of your specialty, but inevitably there will be more you can learn about several parts of your new career. That's why a growing number of salons have devised their own apprenticeship programs or assistant programs that all new hires must complete before becoming full-fledged staff cosmetologists.

The first few years in the salon are paying-your-dues time. Don't expect to become a top stylist your first year. It's been proved time and again that if you treat your first few years in the salon as a learning experience, then you will come out ahead, financially and otherwise, in the long run.

As an assistant, you will need to be patient and open to constant learning. Many salon owners will provide educational opportunities for assistants, such as sending them to seminars or trade shows or paying for continuing education courses. These opportunities help assistants build on what they learned in their training program and what they are experiencing day to day at the salon. If your salon offers such a program, be sure to take advantage of it. If it doesn't have an existing program, talk to your salon owner about establishing one. Small salons may not have a budget for a full-blown education reimbursement program, but they may be able to pay for specific courses or seminars that will help you to become a better employee. Either way, you should work with your supervisor to outline a series of short-term goals that ultimately will help you to become an established hairstylist.

Most of your learning, however, will come from your on-the-job experience. You will observe other stylists at work and learn how they develop relationships with their clients, juggle multiple tasks, contend with last minute cancellations, lousy tips, and how they work with you and the other members of the salon team.

In most salons, assistantships last an average of one year. Two common assistantship programs are described below.

Assistant to Junior Stylist to Senior Stylist

In this type of program, you may spend the first month or two observing and studying. You will be asked to perform basic salon duties like sweeping up or shampooing, but your main goal is to watch the other stylists. You would move from assistant to junior stylist after about six months. At this level, you may assist with hair design—blow-drying, haircolor, simple tints, and chemical processes. You might be given the opportunity to cut and style hair while a senior stylist monitors your work. After a year (sometimes shorter, sometimes longer), when your salon manager feels you are ready, you will move up to become a full-fledged stylist. By this time, you will have observed the salon culture and figured out how you fit in to it.

Apprenticeship

In an apprenticeship program, you would work under the guidance of one stylist or salon professional before becoming a full stylist yourself. This will enable you to build a relationship with that hairstylist's clients, so that they get to know and feel comfortable with you. Typically, you will start out working as a shampooist for the stylist. Then you may assist him or her in haircolor. From there, you will move up to working on all chemical services. As you become more experienced, you will steadily begin to work on clients with less and less input from the stylist.

Regardless of the way the assistant period works at your salon, you need to remember that it is critical to your growth as a beauty professional. Don't become frustrated. Instead, learn all that you can and seize every opportunity to further your development. If you have a positive attitude and you take advantage of the assistant period, you will be ready to thrive in your career as a beauty professional.

Success Strategy

If you're anxious to start working on live heads, recruit your own models for your salon's model night. (If your salon doesn't have one, ask your salon owner to start one—they're great experience for you and great exposure for the salon.) Ask friends, family members, and former fellow students to bring themselves or send their friends in for budget-priced cuts, courtesy of you.

MANAGING WORK RELATIONSHIPS: BASIC RULES

You may not have been aware of it, but you began establishing your professional reputation while you were in your training program. Did you show up to your classes on time? Good, you have a reputation for being responsible. Did you volunteer for your school's hair styling fundraiser? Excellent, you have a reputation for doing more than you have to do. You built on that reputation when you began applying for jobs and participating in job interviews. Your professional reputation is what people think of you in terms of your personality, competence, and attitude. This perception contributes greatly to what coworkers, supervisors, clients, and anyone else you come into professional contact with might say or think about you.

No matter what type of cosmetology specialization you choose to pursue, your success will depend largely on the relationships you develop and cultivate on the job. This refers to how you get along with others, both those you work with and the clients you serve. Making a conscious effort to respect others and ensuring that you're a team player while on the job will help your career immensely.

When it comes to building and maintaining professional relationships, some basic rules apply to any workplace.

Sometimes peace is better than justice

You may be sure you are right about a specific situation. Unfortunately, you may have coworkers who disagree with you. This is a common occurrence in the workplace. Sometimes it will be appropriate to assert your position and convince others to trust your judgment. Your previous track record and reputation will go a long way in helping people to trust your opinions, ideas, and decisions. Just be sure to choose your battles wisely. For instance, go ahead and argue your position if you can prevent a catastrophe. On the other hand, if you are having a debate about an issue of taste or preference, you may want to leave the situation alone or accept the decisions of your superiors. Let your recommendation(s) be known, but do not argue your point relentlessly. Sometimes you will be right and people will not listen to you. Always be open to compromise and be willing to listen to and consider the options and ideas of others.

Don't burn bridges

Think of your career as a long and winding path on which you travel from experience to experience. The people with whom you interact throughout your career are the bridges connecting various portions of your path. You never know how many times you will come upon the same bridge during your journey. If you burn it in a fit of self-righteousness, (by telling off an annoying coworker, for example) an entire portion of your potential path could be closed to you.

Remember: Your professional reputation will follow you throughout your career. It takes years to build a positive reputation, but only one mistake could destroy it. If you wind up acting unprofessionally toward someone, even if you don't ever have contact with that person again, he or she will have contact with many other people and possibly describe you as hard to work with or downright rude. Your work reputation is very important; don't tarnish it by burning your bridges.

Keep work and your social life separate

While it's important to be friendly and form positive relationships with the people you work with, beware of becoming too chummy. Personal relationships can wreak havoc in the workplace, especially if those relationships turn sour. Consider that you might have to rate a friend's job performance, or fire someone you hang out with. If you become friends with a coworker, you may want to have a conversation with him or her to outline what the crossover between your friendship and work relationship will be. Some people refuse to discuss work issues outside of the workplace. Setting boundaries will help your relationship succeed in the long-term.

Success Strategy

If you don't understand something, ask. Your boss may ask you to mix up a color formula you've never heard of, or to operate the phone system you've never worked with. Don't assume you will be able to figure out what he's asking you to do unless you're absolutely sure about it. It's always best to ask a simple clarifying question rather than taking a long time to fill your boss's request. But it is best to ask only once, and then commit the response to memory. No one likes to hear the same questions over and over again. Furthermore, follow instructions to the letter. If something's unclear, ask for clarification.

Managing Your Relationship with Your Boss

A boss is part teacher and part manager, and often (but not always) a salon professional as well. He or she expects you to succeed and will do everything within reason to ensure that you do, but your success ultimately depends on you. As a salon professional, chances are you're a people person: You pick up on their physical or psychological cues. Use your insight to study your boss. Pay attention to what he or she says; watch their manner. It's important that you understand their professional values so you can meet performance expectations.

It's also very important to keep the communication lines open. Talk to your boss about her management style and adjust your expectations to work within that style. For instance, your first boss might like to be hands-on and help you troubleshoot problems. She might want to talk to you at least once a day to hear about your activities. You need to understand that this boss wants to empower you through a mentoring/teaching style.

On the other hand, your boss might want you to call him only if you have a problem. You need to understand that this boss wants to empower you through a hands-off style that lets you find your own solutions. Both bosses may be good managers; they simply have different styles. Understand the value of each style and get the most from it.

Also talk to your boss about *your* career goals. Set goals for six months, one year, three years, and five years. Based on your discussions, you and your boss can create strategies to lead you toward your goals. If you are a people person and an organizer, you might want to move toward a management position and set relevant goals. No matter what you are interested in, make a plan, share it with your boss, and get a few steps closer to achieving your goals.

Dealing with a Difficult Boss

If you're in a situation where you simply don't see eye-to-eye with your boss, you have several options. You can do nothing, live with the situation, hope that it doesn't get worse, and not let your relationship with your boss impact you emotionally, or you can quit your job and seek employment elsewhere. Either of these might appear to be the easiest solution to your problem, but neither will most likely lead to long-term career fulfillment.

Another option is to carefully evaluate your situation and choose to alter your attitude and behavior, and to do whatever it takes to develop a relationship with your boss that evolves around mutual respect. Developing this type of professional relationship doesn't mean you will become best friends with your boss, but it does mean that you should find a way to work together so that you're both happy and productive.

Having an occasional disagreement with a superior is normal, but if your life is being ruined by the actions of a mean or difficult boss, it's up to you to take action and find a solution that you can be happy with.

Know Your Rights

Pregnancy discrimination laws prevent employers from penalizing you because of pregnancy, including loss of pay or job benefits, or even reassigning you to other positions under the pretext of protecting your pregnancy. If you experience a job loss, loss in pay, or loss of position in a company, consult a lawyer immediately. Keep in mind that the Federal Family and Medical Leave Act (FMLA) grants a cumulative 12 weeks of leave in a 12-month period. However, you may be entitled to more leave under state laws or your company plan.

Managing Relationships with Your Coworkers

You will meet many people in the course of your career. Some you will admire; some you will find barely tolerable. For your personal development, you need to find a way to work well with everyone—even if they're not your friends. Acknowledging and accepting someone else's talents and expertise is very different from being their close friend, yet in the workplace, maintaining a professional respect for people you work with will allow everyone to be more productive and successful.

The following are some fundamental rules for fostering positive working relationships with your peers:

> ▶ **Don't gossip about your salon manager, fellow stylists, the receptionist, or anyone else.** Gossip hurts the person being talked about, will inevitably come back to haunt you, and also can make you look like you don't have enough to do.
> ▶ **Foster sharing relationships instead of competitive relationships.** If you experiment with a new hair coloring technique or read an interesting article in a beauty magazine, share the information with the other stylists. A group of people who help each other develop professionally will shine as a team and as individuals. Your salon will develop a more familial atmosphere and clients will have a good feeling when they walk through the door. On the other hand, if you jockey for position and compete over everything, you will miss out on the wealth that you could learn from more experienced stylists (and you will have to work in a competitive, strained salon environment).
> ▶ **Don't become a backstabber, only looking out for yourself.** And never, ever actively steal clients from another stylist. When it comes time for employee evaluations or consideration for a raise, you want to be viewed as a hard working, sincere, honest, team player who does his or her best work in the interest of the salon as a whole.

Your workplace peers can be the greatest pleasure of your job—or your biggest pain. As with your boss, it's best to put your keen observational skills to the test. If you do, you will soon identify the best hairdressers, the hardest workers, the chronic complainers, and the clock-watchers.

It's hard to know where to draw the line with colleagues, particularly if you're fond of them all. A good rule of thumb to remember: They're your coworkers, not your family. Don't get overly involved in their lives. Remember the purpose of your job: To help you develop your career.

Some other tips:

▶ **Always be friendly and professional.** If you're having a bad day (the car broke down, the baby is sick, your tax return was smaller than expected), try to push that aside. Practice treating your coworkers the same way you treat your clients.

▶ **Don't get involved in disputes.** Unless you witness something grossly unethical on the job—and think perhaps the salon owner should be made aware of it—keep quiet. It's a no-win situation otherwise.

▶ **Solve your own conflicts.** Don't get the boss involved unless the situation is so bad that you want to leave your job and you believe the salon owner can do something about the problem. Remember, too, that your salon owner is not likely to promote you to a high-level position unless you exhibit maturity and problem-solving skills. Dragging her into personality disputes will only make her think less of you as a professional.

▶ **Don't let praise go to your head—and don't take criticism to heart.**

▶ **Always behave responsibly.** If your salon owner doesn't want you smoking in the back room, don't. Don't leave the front desk unattended while you go grab a muffin, and never, ever put off grunt work until tomorrow.

▶ **Be approachable.** Have lunch with the group; don't hide in the back room. You want to feel comfortable with your coworkers and you want them to feel comfortable with you. You can learn a lot from each other's experiences. It can only help you in your career to see what goes on in other parts of the salon or spa and a good way to do this is to trade services. For instance, a hairdresser may give a haircut to an esthetician, and an esthetician may reciprocate by giving the hairdresser a facial.

▶ **Treat everyone equally.** You will always have favorite coworkers, just as you will have favorite clients—and others you might half-wish not to have. But you'd feel terribly if the latter clients could sense your dislike; the same goes for your fellow employees.

Managing Your Relationship with Your Receptionist

Your salon's receptionist is perhaps the most important person in the salon. Receptionists are the face salons show to the public; they book appointments, greet guests, match walk-ins to appropriate hairdressers, and generally make sure everything is in order. If you're on commission and the receptionist doesn't schedule you a good number of appointments, your paycheck will suffer. To develop a sound relationship with your salon receptionist, follow these key points:

- ▶ **Be respectful.** A receptionist who feels mistreated, ignored, or snubbed might consciously or subconsciously decide to steer clients away from you.
- ▶ **Be informative.** Let the receptionist know what kind of clients you like and what type of styles you're best at or need to work on so that you're more likely to get clients you're comfortable with.
- ▶ **Be tolerant.** Sometimes it's impossible—due to timing constraints or other factors—to give everyone an equal number of appointments. Some people may get stuck doing all haircuts one day, while someone else gets three chemical services at twice the revenue. Also, the receptionist must always abide by the wishes of the client. If the client must have stylist X, then the client will get him—whether it's your turn or not.
- ▶ **Know your schedule.** Time your services to maximize your efficiency, but be realistic about how long it will take you to finish a client. You don't want to keep a client waiting. If you're done with a client earlier than expected, alert the receptionist so walk-ins can be sent your way.
- ▶ **Verbalize problems.** If you don't tell the receptionist that you're unhappy about something, how do you expect it to change? Being proactive can prevent a difficult situation from becoming really difficult.

Managing Your Time

You will most likely find that the workplace environment is more hectic than school was, so you will need to manage your time effectively to make the most of your workweek. Here are some tips for juggling your tasks and managing your time.

▶ **Know the requirements of your job and what your boss expects of you.** Define your role and know what is expected of you on a daily basis. Does your boss want you to promote styling products at the end of every appointment? You need to know this in order to do it.

▶ **Don't get trapped by interruptions and time wasters.** Every job is subject to time wasters. If you work with a social, chatty person, don't let yourself be distracted or interrupted. Your client doesn't want to feel that your conversation with the shampooist is more important than her highlights.

▶ **Keep a day planner.** Remember this tool from job hunting? Identify one place where you write everything down, whether it is a formal day planner or a spiral notebook. Are you always running late for appointments? Do the items on your daily to-do list never seem to get done fast enough? Do you feel that you don't have any spare time to learn and develop new skills? If there is never enough time in your day to meet your personal and professional obligations, you could be lacking important time management skills.

Learning time management skills won't add more hours to the work day, but it will allow you to use all of your time more productively, reduce the stress in your life, better focus on what's important, and ultimately get more done faster.

Get a day planner and then spend a few days carefully analyzing how you spend your time. Determine what takes up the majority of your time, but diminishes your productivity. Also, by writing down your priorities, you will be able to schedule your time more efficiently. Learning to better manage your time will boost your productivity, which will ultimately make you more valuable to an employer, putting you in a better position to eventually receive a raise or promotion.

Managing Life and a Job

When you are at work every day all week long, it becomes difficult to get your *life tasks* done. Here are some tips to help you integrate your job with your life.

▶ **Make to-do lists and prioritize the tasks you need to accomplish.**
Keep a list of things you need to do, buy, return, pick up, and drop off.
A day planner is the best place to keep such a list. If you don't have a
day planner, carry a notebook with you from home to work and back
again. Organize your list according to places you will stop. Keep grocery items on one list, pharmacy items on another, dry cleaning on a
third, etc. Cross things off the lists when you have finished them so you
can see what you have to do at a glance.

▶ **Use your lunch hour to run errands at least once a week.** Identify
resources that are close to your work for things you can do during your
lunch hour—doctor, dentist, dry cleaner, shoe repair, car repair, hard-
ware store, and so on.

▶ **Use the commute between home and work to take care of other
errands, such as stopping at gas station and the grocery store.**

Money Saving Tips

In your first cosmetology job, because your pay is not what it soon will be, it may be hard
to keep expenses from outpacing your income. Here some tips to help you start saving
money:

▶ Make your own coffee in the morning rather than stopping at the local coffee shop,
and eat breakfast at home.

▶ Bring your lunch.

▶ When grocery shopping, make a list beforehand and stick to it. If you have a plan
going in, you will be less likely to purchase impulse (and often expensive) items.

▶ If your salon offers a 401(k) plan, join up as soon as possible and put in as much
of your salary as you can. You will save in taxes immediately and you will be building for your retirement.

▶ Find out if your salon offers direct deposit of paychecks. If it does, choose to have
either a percent or set amount ($25 per paycheck, for example) deposited into
your savings account.

▶ Swap beauty services with other stylists.

▶ Make a budget with short-term and long-term saving goals.

▶ Pay off your debt. Start with lenders that charge the highest interest (department
store credit cards are notorious for their high interest rates) and work your way
down to the lowest interest.

SURVIVING YOUR FIRST WEEKS AT A NEW JOB

For many job seekers, the stress involved with finding new job opportunities, sending out resumes, participating in interviews, and dealing with all of the other hassles involved with finding employment can be emotionally draining. Thus, it makes perfect sense that most people experience a huge sense of relief once they're actually offered a new job, conduct a successful salary negotiation, and then accept a new position.

The problem is, as soon as some people show up for their first day of work, the stress associated with beginning a new job kicks in, which could make the first few weeks at a new job unpleasant. Stepping into a new job situation can be difficult. It often involves a major change in your daily routine, getting to know an entirely new group of people, and learning the policies and procedures of your new employer.

You also need to learn about the underlying office politics that play a major role in any work environment, and determine exactly what is expected of you in terms of job performance. It's necessary to determine exactly how you fit in the operation of the salon and be willing to adapt your work habits to meet the needs of the employer.

Hopefully, before accepting your job, you did research to learn about the salon and what you'd be doing there, so you're confident you've found the right job for you. If you go into a new job knowing there's a good chance you're going to enjoy it, the stress associated with starting the job will be greatly diminished, since much of the stress you'd typically feel would be in anticipation of entering into an unknown situation.

Adapting to a new work situation happens instantaneously for some, but for others could take up to three or four weeks. As an assistant, you will be learning constantly, so there will be adjustments for you to make throughout your first year. During this time, be open-minded and try to maintain a positive attitude, no matter how unhappy or stressed out you are. Until some time has passed, it's difficult to tell if you simply accepted the wrong job, or if you're experiencing the new job acclimation process, which is normal. Unless you're absolutely sure you've made the wrong job decision by accepting your job after a week or two, stick it out for at least a month before making the decision to quit if you're unhappy.

During your first few weeks at a new job, there are several things you can do to help yourself and your coworkers become more comfortable. First, instead of confronting people who may give you a difficult time, try to fit in right from the start by being friendly toward everyone. Also, ask questions to demonstrate a desire to learn how things are done, and whenever possible, attempt to strike up non-work-related conversations, especially during lunch or break periods. This will help you get to know the people you're working with on a personal level.

Always think of a new job as providing a new set of exciting opportunities and a chance to start fresh. By taking control of your life, you can seek out and pursue those opportunities that will lead to career advancement and happiness. You must, however, face these opportunities with the proper mindset and be willing to work hard for what you want. Never allow the fear of failing to hold you back as you begin to take advantage of the opportunities your new job has to offer.

If you begin your new job determined to be open-minded, professional, friendly, persistent, and flexible, chances are you will adapt quickly and soon be accepted by your new coworkers.

IMPROVING YOUR CHANCES FOR SUCCESS

You want to love what you do. Unfortunately, there are many challenges that you will face along the way that can hinder your success. One of the biggest challenges for salon professionals—at any level—is building and sustaining a clientele. This is where some strategic business thinking (which you may or may not have received in beauty school) comes in handy.

Strategic thinking means having an eye on your long-term goal and then clearing a path to obtain it. After working in a salon environment for a year or two, you probably have a good idea of what you'd ultimately like to do in the world of beauty. Now it's time to put your own career plan into effect.

Setting Goals

If you don't know where you are going, how can you get there? Establishing what you want out of your career and working toward that goal will ensure that you reach it. It is also a good way to combat the boredom that consumes many cosmetologists after the initial thrill of their new career wears off. Don't tell yourself that you can't do something; you will have plenty of people telling you the same thing! Instead, think about what will fulfill you.

Make an outline of both long-term and short-term goals. It's essential to know yourself—what makes you happy and what attracted you to the beauty business in the first place. Then let yourself dream: Picture yourself owning a 10,000-square-foot salon. It may seem like pie-in-the-sky stuff, but it will help you to discover where your interests lie.

Ascertain whether your strengths mesh with your interests. Generally they do—people like what they're good at—but if they don't, now is the time to rethink your goals.

Once you've refined your goal, outline the steps you must take to make it a reality. Then prioritize them and develop a time frame for accomplishing those steps. Sometimes, working on this with a partner—a colleague or friend—can help keep you both motivated. A good mentor can be extremely helpful. Finding one is described in the section below.

If you fall short of a specific goal, don't feel that you've failed or that the goal is unreachable. It's simply a goal deferred. Pat yourself on the back for coming so close. Then re-strategize to make sure that next time you will achieve what you want.

Learn from a Mentor

A mentor is someone you identify as successful and with whom you create a sort of teacher-student relationship in order to learn from his or her experiences. Choose your mentor based on what is important to you and on how you define success. For example, if you want to open your own salon in the future, you would want a mentor who has successfully opened a salon. Similarly, if your goal is to balance a family and a career, look for someone who seems to do this well. Enter into the relationship intending to observe your mentor carefully and ask many questions.

You will want to find a mentor with advanced knowledge of the beauty industry who can teach you skills, direct your path for ongoing learning, and help you develop a successful career path. Although each mentoring situation is different, you often can learn the following from a mentor:

▶ How to design a career plan
▶ How to set incremental goals
▶ Client relationship skills and how to build a loyal clientele
▶ What to expect in your salon culture
▶ How to communicate with your salon manager, receptionist, and other stylists
▶ Inside information on other local salons (great for when you are looking for a new job!)
▶ Problem-solving skills
▶ Pros and cons of various product lines
▶ Trends in the beauty industry
▶ Which beauty magazines are best
▶ Which conferences/seminars/classes you should attend

How to Connect with a Mentor

Don't just wait for your fairy godmother to appear and provide you with a mentor; actively search for one. A mentor can be anyone from a salon owner to a fellow stylist. When looking for a good mentor you shouldn't just look for title, years in the beauty industry, or years with your salon. You want to find a cosmetologist with knowledge and experience related to your goals. Most important, that person must be willing to help you and share information.

There are many ways to find a mentor. Since you probably will be looking for a mentor when you start your new job, you won't know many people at the company. Try these techniques for identifying possible mentors:

▶ **Ask your salon manager or owner to recommend someone.** Let them know that you are proactively trying to improve yourself through a mentor. This actually helps you in two ways. First, it helps you find an appropriate mentor based on your salon environment. Second, it lets your boss know that you are serious about your career and your personal development.

▶ **Observe people.** You can learn a lot this way. When asked a question, do they take the time to help you find a resolution or do they point you toward someone else who can help you? The one who takes the time to help you resolve your question is the better choice for a mentor. How does the potential mentor resolve problems? In a calm manner? Do problems get resolved? If so, you've found a good candidate.

▶ **Listen to people who admire your potential mentor.** What qualities do they admire? Do the admirable qualities coincide with your values and goals? If you need to learn conflict-resolution skills, you probably shouldn't consider a mentor who is admired for a forceful, aggressive style. Instead, look for someone people describe as fair, calm, and easy to work with.

Marketing Yourself

Marketing and promotion are key elements for any beauty professional's success. You want people to think of you first when they are getting ready to make a beauty appointment. One of the first steps you should take is to invest in your image. You never have a second chance to make a first impression, so dress for respect.

Your business card is an essential but inexpensive marketing tool. It should be professionally designed and distinctive. (If your salon has standard cards for everyone, stay within those parameters.) Have at least 2,000 printed up, and always carry them with you. Give them to each new client, the cashier at your supermarket, the local librarian, your neighbor, and all of your friends and family members. Everyone is a potential client.

One marketing strategy that may take a little more of your time but will yield huge rewards is to get involved with the business of the salon. Offer to head up the salon's promotions, charitable events, fashion shows, and other special events. You will not only learn terrific team-building skills, but you will also gain many new clients through the events you organize. Similarly, you should do some business-to-business networking. Get out of the salon at least once or twice a month to meet new people in your community. If your salon belongs to the local Chamber of Commerce, ask your salon owner if you may attend some of the business-to-business events and functions with him or her.

An easier strategy but one with a cost involved is to develop client referral programs. One way to do this is to offer your clients three extra business cards; ask them to print their name on the back and give the cards to friends or coworkers. Then, if any of their referrals come to the salon, they and their friend will each receive $5 off their next service. (Again, your salon may have a similar program in place. If it doesn't, it should—so why not suggest it?)

If your salon owner is comfortable with the idea, call your new clients a week or so after their first salon visit to see how they felt about their service. Follow-up is key to client retention—and to be truly successful, you need to retain a high percentage of your first-time clients. If they're dissatisfied, always offer to perform a corrective service at no charge.

Don't forget to read beauty trade and consumer fashion magazines. Trade magazines are a great source of marketing tips and success stories you can learn from, and both trade and fashion magazines offer information on the latest trends in hair, makeup, nailcare, and skincare as well as cultural information that will keep you on the cutting edge and enable you to be a *total* image consultant to your clients.

How to Hold a Cut-a-thon

A cut-a-thon is a great way to become active in the community and gain local exposure. To help you get started, here is a list based on successful cut-a-thons held by Randy Currie, who owns Currie Hair Skin and Nails salon (he has organized an average of two cut-a-thons a year for the past five years) and Kristen Crook of the Hair Cuttery chain (75 of its nearly 800 salons worldwide hold one every year):

▶ Pick a good cause. "The most successful cut-a-thons benefit a cause that the community has a direct interest in," says Crook. For example, donating money to someone whose house has burnt down or to a local charity is something everyone can relate to. If you're not sure what organizations are in your area, check with your Chamber of Commerce.

▶ Make sure you know where the money is going. "Even charities have been known to misuse funds on occasion," notes Currie. So before you select a cause, sit down with representatives from the organization you want to work with and ask exactly how the money will be used.

▶ Pick a time and day for the event. Currie and Hair Cuttery both hold cut-a-thons during non-working hours, either on a Sunday or in the evenings after the salon closes. This way they're not losing money.

▶ Start planning early. "There is no such thing as too early to start planning an in-salon event," says Crook. Currie gets the ball rolling six weeks prior to an event.

▶ Get everyone involved. Explain to stylists that they'll have an opportunity to gain new clients while helping a worthy cause.

▶ Create committees. Not only does this help to spread around all the work, it's a good way to get stylists excited.

▶ Determine your promotional strategy for the event. This includes asking the organization you're supporting to help you promote your cut-a-thon, advertising the event in local newspapers, and mailing announcements to attendees of any previous cut-a-thons.

▶ Work the public relations angle. Call the local media before and after cut-a-thons. "When it's a charity event, the local newspapers usually have no problem giving you coverage," notes Currie.

▶ Give customers a reason to come. "We have the most success when we do half-price cuts," reports Crook. "There has to be something in it for the clients." Another way to entice people is with a raffle. Currie gets local stores and his distributor to donate gift certificates and products, all of which are raffled off during the event.

▶ Give your staff a dress code. Even though cut-a-thons are meant to be fun, you and your staff should look professional if you want customers to leave with a good impression. Currie and Crook both suggest making up T-shirts for the event and asking the staff to wear these with black pants.

▶ Make a list of things you will want available the day of the event. This should include business cards, price menus, goodie bags, coupons, and haircare products. You will also want to have a guestbook that customers can sign as they come in so you can build your mailing list.

▶ Once the event is over, be sure to review it in your head and with your staff. By doing a recap, you will learn from your experience so you can make the next one even better.

Source: Excerpted and reprinted with permission of Chantel Todé Jensen and behindthechair.com (www.behindthechair.com)

Using the Media

One of the most effective ways to promote yourself and your skills is through the media. Fortunately, you work in an industry with more than its share of publications, both trade and consumer. There's also plenty of beauty and fashion information on cable and broadcast television. Not everyone can be Vidal Sassoon or Bobbi Brown, but you can still get the media to pay attention to your story. Here are some suggestions:

▶ **Issue press releases to local and national media outlets, using the salon's letterhead.** You can use a press release to announce a salon event or predict the haircolors clients will want next season. Each press release should be succinct, with a contact name and phone number (yours) readily visible. As with your resume, make sure you and someone else proofread the press release before sending it out.

▶ **Consider the type of coverage you want.** If you're analyzing a style trend, magazines and newspapers are probably your best bet. If you want some coverage for a cut-a-thon the salon is hosting, then send the press release to the local media, especially TV. You never know—they may send over a camera crew.

▶ **Keep track of press release recipients and follow up with a phone call confirming receipt.** Always address your press releases to a specific person; ask your salon's receptionist to do some detective work over the phone to help you in this task, and make sure the names are spelled correctly.

▶ **If you want post-event coverage from a magazine, include photos.** You should always take photos at any event in which your salon participates. Be sure to provide caption information, along with the five *W*'s and the *H* (*Who, What, Where, When, Why*, and *How*), in each press release. Even if you never make the papers, you can put together a photo collage to hang on the wall. It will tell clients that the salon is an integral part of the community.

▶ **Make yourself available for comment.** For instance, the morning after the Academy Awards, fax your own hit-or-miss evaluation of the evening's hairstyles and fashions to members of the media. Do the same thing seasonally during the fashion shows in London, Milan, Paris, and New York. (Thanks to cable television, the images from these events are now available instantly, so it's best to strike early.) Explain why, in your opinion, the styles seen on the runway will be a hit or a miss with real-life clients. If you position yourself as an expert on trends, particularly as they relate to fashion and to celebrities, editors will definitely give you a call.

▶ **Offer to contribute a style column to your local newspaper.** In it you can respond to questions from readers. (For example, "What's the best way to avoid frizzies when the weather gets hot and humid?" "What's the difference between permanent and semipermanent haircolor?")

▶ **Do your own photo shoots.** If you want your creative work published in a magazine, you will have to show the editor what you are capable of. In the beginning, you will have to set up your own photo shoots and send the resulting photos (along with a resume and cover letter describing why they should look at your work) to the editor. Always get your models to sign a model release form (a document giving you permission to reproduce their pictures for publication), or magazines will not publish your pictures. They don't want a lawsuit on their hands.

▶ **Take constructive criticism.** If you want to know why your work isn't being published, ask—in a professional, non-aggressive way. You may not be selecting the proper models or the right backgrounds, or you may be behind trend. Beauty is such a fast-moving industry that you need to be ahead of the curve, anticipating what styles people will be wearing before they wear them.

▶ **Make yourself familiar with all of the media outlets to which you are sending releases.** Subscribe to the magazines, watch the television shows, and listen to the radio. The more informed you are, the better your pitch, or story idea, will sound to the appropriate editor or reporter.

Other points to remember: Always label photographs; send slides or transparencies, not prints; provide all necessary credit information; and share your ideas and concepts in an accompanying note. Send duplicates, not originals; most magazines will not return the photos you send them. (Remember, they probably receive dozens per day.)

If you're serious about photo shoots, take a photography class. Even if you don't take the photos yourself, you will learn what goes into making a picture. Look into taking a class on doing photo shoots; they're offered by dozens of beauty-industry image companies. You will get valuable tips on lighting, composition, what makes a good model, how to think two-dimensionally for the camera, and other good information.

Networking

Being able to effectively communicate what you and your business are about is not just a plus, it's essential. Knowing how to approach people at parties, at trade shows, and on your local jogging track can open doors to new business.

Here are some tips for meeting new people:

▶ **Do your homework.** Find out who is sponsoring the event and who is attending.
▶ **Develop a positive attitude.** A bit of enthusiasm and a smile go a long way.
▶ **Focus on the benefits.** Are you meeting with people to drum up more business? To be visible among your peers? To learn the latest trends?
▶ **Plan your introduction.** Remember, you want to tell people who you are and give them a pleasant impression of you.
▶ **Bring your business cards.** This is a must. In fact, you should carry them with you wherever you go.
▶ **Prepare your small talk.** If you have trouble, comment on the food, the weather—anything to break the ice.
▶ **When meeting people, look them in the eye, smile, and firmly shake hands.** This will convey a sense of self-confidence.

Pushing Products

Working in a salon isn't simply about performing services for clients. It's also about helping them maximize their style even when they're not in the salon. To do this, they need at-home care products—and you should be selling them.

You're probably thinking, "I'm not a salesperson, I'm an artist!" But as creative as you are, your first and foremost job in the salon is servicing clients, and this means keeping them looking their best.

Plus, retailing makes great business sense. Salon owners offer generous commission on retail items in an effort to encourage their sale. You can easily make an extra $100 a day just by selling shampoo and conditioner to your clients. That figure can double if you focus on styling aids too.

Be sure to avoid retail killers such as assessing clients' ability to afford products based on their appearance, being afraid that the client will say no, not having the courage to close the sale, or not listening and not communicating.

Instead of falling into these traps, try using the following techniques:

▶ **Keep the products visible at your station.**

▶ **Discuss products as you're using them.** Explain why they're particularly good for that client's hair.

▶ **Show the client how to use the product.** Many clients complain that they don't know how to use a product—for instance, what constitutes a dab of gel or how gel should be worked into the hair.

▶ **Encourage clients to touch and smell the product.** Fragrance is the single biggest selling trigger for personal care products.

▶ **Give out trial-size samples to new clients—you're likely to get them hooked.**

JUST THE FACTS

Average salon prices:

Manicure: $14.18

Pedicure: $27.58

Full Set: $39.64

Fill: $21.99

Source: Nails Magazine

The Importance of Consultations

When you start at a salon, your salon owner or manager most likely will train you in the salon's specific consultation technique, but it never hurts to know the basics. The consultation is key because it's an icebreaker—your chance to size up the client's wants, needs, and lifestyle. It's also the primary way to get new clients to relax in your chair. Having a great chairside manner will take you a long way. Here are some general questions to open with:

▶ "Is this your first time at the salon?"

▶ "What do you do for a living?"

▶ "What do you like about your hair?"

▶ "What don't you like?"

▶ "Why did you leave your last salon?" (ask of a new client only)

▶ "What products do you use?"

▶ "What styling tools (blow dryer, curling iron) do you use?"

▶ "Is there anything else I should know?"

This last question is crucial. If clients don't know how to respond, prompt them by asking, "Do you color your hair? Do you take any medications that I should know about? Are you looking for a big change or just small adjustments?"

During the consultation it's critical to maintain eye contact. Speak only to the client—make him or her feel like the only person in the world. Be tactful. (For instance, don't point out obvious gray hair.) Show examples in the form of swatches and photos. If the client brings in a photo, be courteous and ask them to specify what they like about the style in the photo.

Sometimes, no matter how smoothly you handle the consultation, it's just not easy to communicate with a client. For instance, you may have an idea for a cut and persuade the client to try it, but he or she may start get antsy as you proceed. In such cases, stop cutting and explain to the client what you're doing and why. Don't proceed too quickly. Work efficiently, but never make it difficult for clients to voice their opinion.

Supporting Your Community

Getting involved with the community has always been a part of salon culture. It also enables you to meet people and become known. Suggest that your salon do one or more of the following, and volunteer to lead the projects:

▶ **Hold makeover nights.** Invite clients to come in and watch a makeover or two. Demonstrate styling tips for at-home use, such as how to blow-dry hair using a round brush.

▶ **Participate in fundraisers for charities.** In communities all across the United States there are local and national fundraisers with which it is easy to get involved. For example, the Komen Race for the Cure series (a community-based fundraising 5K run/walk for breast cancer research) holds events in many cities, large and small, across the country. Getting your clients and fellow staff members to participate is a great way to foster a sense of community within your salon—especially if you go the extra mile and get T-shirts printed with your salon logo for them all to wear.

▶ **Put on a fashion show.** Team up with the local women's association, local merchants, and department stores. Charge a nominal fee, with all proceeds going to the local women's shelter or another worthy recipient.

▶ **Collect money, clothing, or food for the needy.** You can do this either year-round or at the holidays.

▶ **Host a bridal fair.** In the spring, display new styles for hair and gowns, using local brides-to-be as models. (Check your local newspaper's engagement listings for names.) Contact your local bridal shops for the gowns and florists for the bouquets. You can contact local wedding photographers to get them involved, too. (And, don't forget to ask for copies of the photos—you will definitely want to send a press release to your local papers for this event.)

▶ **Give something back to the industry.** Volunteer to speak at your beauty school, sharing your experiences with new students. Offer to become a role model for the Cosmetology Advancement Foundation, traveling to vocational and secondary schools in your area to promote the value of a cosmetology career.

There are existing programs that offer a wonderful way for beauty professionals to volunteer their services. Two well-known programs are listed here:

▶ **Look Good . . . Feel Better.** This program is a way for beauty professionals to donate their time and services to help the community, and grow artistically as well. LGFB is the brainchild of the National Cancer Society and provides beauty consultations and support to women recovering from cancer. You can work with styling wigs or teach women how to apply their camouflage makeup or care for their skin so they'll feel better about themselves during this traumatic time in their lives. Many local chapters of the National

Cosmetology Association are supporters of this program. To find out more about this worthy program, visit their website at www.lookgoodfeelbetter.org.

▶ **Work Your Image!** Like the Look Good . . . Feel Better program, this is another way for you to grow while giving back to the community and people who need your services. Work Your Image! helps displaced homemakers, single parents, welfare recipients, and other women in transition improve their image so they make their best first impression as they compete in the job market. This program is the project of the Cosmetic, Toiletry and Fragrance Association and Women Work! The National Network for Women's Employment. To learn how you can get involved, visit www.womenwork.org or www.ctfa.org

Cross-Promoting Services

In an age when salons are offering more and more types of beauty services—and clients seem to want one-stop beauty shopping—everybody benefits by careful cross-promoting. This simply means telling your clients about the benefits of other services in the salon, and sometimes even giving them a free sample.

For instance, if you're an esthetician, you might want to mention to your clients that there are plenty of hair stylists available to shampoo and blow-dry their hair if they want it styled to complement their glowing skin. Or you can mention that the salon's makeup artist is very talented and is available for consultations. If you're a hairdresser, you can tell clients about the terrific new nail technician and offer a complimentary hand massage or nail buff while clients are waiting for their color to process.

Clients usually respond well to careful cross-promotion. If a client in your chair seems particularly edgy, take the opportunity to extol the talents of the new massage therapist.

Many salons encourage their staff members to cross-promote by giving them a percentage or commission on referrals to other areas of the salon. And think of the goodwill you can generate among your colleagues if they're constantly getting referrals from you. Not to mention the opportunities you will have to sharpen your skills if they do likewise.

MAKING THE MOST OF TRADE SHOWS

The beauty industry loves trade shows such as New York's annual International Beauty Show. Thousands of manufacturers from every segment of the beauty industry come to these events to sell products, offer education, and meet their customers—you. The shows are a valuable resource for fledgling beauty pros. Before you go, consider these tips:

▶ **Make a plan and follow it.** Research the show in advance: Find out which educators, platform artists (people who demonstrate techniques on models), and exhibitors will be there; check out the travel packages. Make sure you give yourself enough time to cover everything.

▶ **Divvy up the work.** If your coworkers are also attending, split up so you can cover more ground. Then take notes and report back to the group on the areas you were responsible for.

▶ **Arrive early.** It's always less crowded first thing in the morning.

▶ **Bring a camera.** Document new styles and techniques for your coworkers and clients.

▶ **Dress in layers.** A crowded show floor can get hot.

▶ **Bring a big bag.** There'll be a lot of new products that you will want to buy—and plenty of samples, too.

▶ **Wear comfortable shoes.** Your feet will thank you later. Nothing will make you more miserable than sore feet.

OTHER CAREER OPTIONS

Booth-Renting

Once you have established yourself as a stylist, you may want to try to work for yourself. One way to do that is to rent a booth at an existing salon. As explained in Chapter 1, booth renters operate as independent contractors and pay a percentage of their gross, or a flat fee, to the salon owner for the space they rent within a salon. Sometimes, you will be able to move into this situation at your current salon. You will have to investigate the situation with your salon owner.

The Insurance Question

If you decide to rent space in a salon or work at home, you need to confront the question of insurance—not just medical, but liability and malpractice as well. Just one injured or dissatisfied client may lead to financial ruin if you're uninsured.

Some salon owners' policies provide coverage for everyone who works at their location. Others let the independent cosmetologist buy in for comprehensive business coverage on the premises. Policies may also cover those who rent space or have a home workplace. Nail down the details before you work on your first client.

Legal Issues

If you're an independent contractor (booth renter), you need to take special care with taxes. To protect yourself, keep accurate records that document the income you list on your return:

▶ Tie your records to your appointment book.

▶ Keep track of your business expenses (they are deductible).

▶ Pay your business expenses with checks.

▶ Keep records of all money received and deposited—including tips. If you misrepresent your income by more than 20%, you may be found guilty of fraud and subjected to substantial penalties.

▶ Pay your estimated taxes quarterly. You can get the appropriate forms from your accountant or directly from the IRS.

▶ Provide the IRS form 1099-MISC to your salon owner or landlord. It should show the amount of rent you paid; the owner is obligated to pay taxes on the equipment.

Booth Renter Checklist

1. Make sure you have a written agreement with the salon owner. It should set limits on your arrangement, and it should be renewed annually. If you work for more than a year without one, the IRS may determine that you're an employee of the salon. Your agreement may be terminated by written notice; an independent contractor cannot be fired at will.

2. Be aware that independent contractors cannot be required to work specific hours or days, attend seminars or meetings, submit reports, or wear a uniform or salon logo.
3. An area of the salon should be designated as your own.
4. You must provide your own tools, equipment, and supplies.
5. You should have business cards and a business checking account to pay all your operating expenses.
6. You should have your own sales tax number if you sell retail products to your clients.

BEYOND THE SALON

At some point you may decide that although you still love cosmetology, you don't want to practice in a salon environment anymore. That's fine: There are plenty of opportunities in other areas.

Specialization

Sometimes you simply need to define what you like most about your job and what you like least, and then concentrate on the former. A growing number of salon professionals are choosing specialties within hairdressing. Some are principally haircutters and some decide to concentrate on chemical services—relaxers, permanent waves, and haircolor services.

Platform Artist or Educator

Cosmetology is a very visual field, and education at trade shows often features hairdressers' work shown on models. If you're interested in creating fashion-forward looks or like the fast-paced energy of beauty shows, this could be the niche for you.

Companies rely on individuals or teams not only to show how their products work but also to create beautiful styles using them. The hope is that these styles will inspire cosmetologists in the audience, who will then take their new knowledge back to the salon and share it with their clients, recommending those products used at the show. If you're comfortable in front of an audience, speak well, and like to collaborate, then this could be a great career path for you.

If you decide that platform work or education is something you'd like to do, forge a relationship with your distributors—attend their classes, ask questions, and become an expert on the various product lines. If you have a particular favorite, approach the distributor about helping out at the educational events it hosts. Once you've got a few classes under your belt, discuss becoming a regional educator. Good platform presenters are invaluable to a distributor or manufacturer; platform presentations are one of the best ways to communicate a product's benefits in a way that hairdressers can relate to.

Good regional educators are often promoted to national artistic teams for major manufacturers, affording opportunities to travel extensively, collaborate with like-minded artists, and gain tremendous visibility within the beauty industry.

When you work for a company, your compensation will depend on your experience and your level of commitment. Some companies hire artists on a monthly retainer. Others may want you to work sporadically, at trade shows, so you will be paid on a per-project basis. Such jobs usually go to pros with several years of salon experience who have made a name for themselves through their own photo shoots—which they send to companies to increase their own visibility.

A few high-profile artists are employed full-time by product manufacturers to produce photo shoots, test products, and the like; their salaries can run well into the six figures. But these jobs are usually open only to people with many years of experience and an extensive body of work.

Photo Session Hairstylists

Photo session hairstylists are sometimes treated as minor celebrities—they have the most-desired positions in the beauty industry. The more renowned include Frederic Fekkai (who now has not only a successful line of hair products, but handbags as well), Oribe, Orlando Pita, John Sahag, and Sam McKnight. Many of these hairdressers not only do photo work but also put in hours behind the chair.

As mentioned in Chapter 1, photo session work is very difficult to get. If you're serious about it, you first need to move to a major metropolitan area—Los Angeles, Miami, and New York have the vast majority of agencies. Don't embark on this plan without an extensive portfolio of test shots (shoots you did with similarly inexperienced but ambitious photographers and makeup artists) that demonstrate your skills. Circulate your book to the big agencies and offer to assist their major hairdressers (or makeup artists) on shoots *gratis*. Learning from a master can really send you on your way—particularly if he or she likes your work.

It's important to remember that advertising work pays far better than editorial work, although the latter is more prestigious. Plan to repeat your dues-paying years if you're serious about getting into session styling.

The Day Spa Option

Over the past few years, day spas have become the hottest growth area in the beauty industry. Day spas offer full-service hair, nails, and skincare along with more traditional spa fare such as massage, hydrotherapy, and body treatments. Generally speaking, state licenses are required only for massage therapists; other treatments can be done by anyone, but it's best to take advanced education classes to learn more. Spa technicians exhibit many of the same skills as hairdressers—patience, listening, understanding, and healing. Spas are great avenues of cross-promotion for other beauty services as well. If you're interested in developing more than one area of expertise in beauty, then working in a day spa may be for you.

Spa Stats

According to the International Spa Association, there are approximately 5,700 spas in the United States and 75% of them are day spas. The number of new day spas in the United States has increased 127% since 1994. That's good news for cosmetologists looking for a career in the spa industry.

The Spa Environment

Day spas provide jobs for massage therapists, electrologists, estheticians, and nail technicians. The first thing you need to know about a spa is that it operates at a much slower pace than a salon. Spa clients are looking for a relaxed, peaceful, stress-free environment. Your demeanor has to be relaxed, and you should speak in a quiet voice. Clients do want to have the same sense of confidence in you that they have in their hairdresser, so you need to come off as if you trust your own abilities.

Most salon owners will look to hire professionals with previous experience. That's simply because you can be a great massage therapist coming out of school, but if you've already worked on two hundred bodies, you're going to be that much better. The most important thing is to get your hands on as many clients as possible to improve your skills.

Success Strategy

A key to day spa success is learning how to work within a time frame. You need to keep your services on schedule. Just as important is your professionalism—it is the key aspect of your career and it will help you earn a lot of money in the long run. This includes developing a sound work ethic early in your career. For instance, calling in sick is the last thing you should do. If you're just burned out, ask your boss for a day off. But don't call in sick and stick the spa owner with eight appointments to fill that day.

Salon Management

After a few years behind the chair or at the nail station, you may decide that although you want to remain in the salon, you don't want to be a service technician any longer. A growing number of schools offer salon-management educational tracks for people who are intrigued by the nuts-and-bolts of running a business. These classes provide insight into profit-and-loss statements; how to manage overhead; how to cost out your revenue per square foot; how to hire, fire, and discipline employees; and other dollars-and-cents issues. Check your advanced-education facilities nearby; more and more of them are responding to the need for such basic business education.

To succeed as a salon manager, you need excellent communication skills—not only with clients but also with staff. You need to know how to step into their shoes and think about how you would want to be treated if you were in their position. You also need to be knowledgeable about what's going on in the world, and in particular the world of your usual clients. Customer service, however, is the most important thing. You want to be seen as someone who cares about the client and is there to serve, but isn't beneath them.

High Seas Beauty

The growing demand for beauty services that pamper and de-stress has rendered the salon and spa essential parts of any cruise ship. Hundreds of young salon professionals have decided they want to work in the beauty field and travel while they're at it. An obvious benefit of this type of work is that you will get to do what you love and see the world at the same time.

If you are interested in this option, start by visiting the Steiner Leisure website at www.steinerleisure.com. They operate spas on over a hundred cruise ships; their salons are found on every major commercial cruise ship. The company hires licensed professionals with two years of experience to work in their facilities. This is typical of the industry. Also typical are three-, six-, or 12-month contracts and up to 12-hour days.

Working in Theater, Film, and Television

This work is notoriously difficult to get; it's largely a matter of who you know. But tenacity can prevail so you should try sending your portfolio to show producers, offering to work for no pay at first, and networking with photographers to do shoots for credit only.

Labor unions are another complicating factor, however. Many shows won't hire you unless you are a union member, but if you can manage to win the favor of an influential performer, that becomes less of an issue.

If you're interested in joining a union, here are some sample prerequisites from Local 798 of the Makeup and Hairdressers Union, which has jurisdiction from Maine to Florida.

▶ You must choose either the hair or makeup category. You can't do both.
▶ The union's screening committee reviews resumes every six months or so. They are looking for artists with theatrical experience, whether in films, commercials, television, or theater.
▶ If the committee members like your resume, they'll call you. You will need to provide proof of employment for at least six months of the past three years. (Proof meaning pay stubs or W-2 tax forms.)
▶ If you meet those requirements, you will be asked to take a written test and a practical test, for which you will have to supply your own models. If you pass, then the union's executive board will approve you.

On the West Coast, Local 706 for motion pictures and television also requires that you work 60 days a year for three years. To prove you've done so, you need your pay stubs and letters from the payroll production company. (The work can be in television or film only.) Also, you can only work in Los Angeles County. If you get into the union, you're eligible for motion picture guild health benefits, plus you will earn the union scale rate. According to the union, production companies employ quite a bit of non-union labor, so your best bet to get started is to subscribe to the trade papers *Daily Variety* and *The Hollywood Reporter* and scour the classified ads.

Distributor or Manufacturer's Rep

A great many beauty professionals go this route, which involves being an employee or a contract worker for a distributor or a product company. Distributors are the middlemen in the beauty industry—they make sales calls on salons and supply them with the products, equipment, and tools they need. Some distributors carry one line of products only; others may carry several dozen. For example, say a company distributes Aveda; it has exclusive rights to do so in your area. You won't find any other distributors that carry that line.

Distributors are manufacturers' links to salons in other ways as well. Salon employees and owners give them feedback on new products, trends, and business developments. They ask distributors for assistance in marketing and for help in figuring out what new services to offer.

Former salon workers often make great distributors because they know where the salon is coming from. They are intimately acquainted with salon culture and know what's needed. Working for a progressive distributor, you can help shape its offerings to better meet the demands of today's salons and barber shops.

Protecting Yourself from Sexual Harassment

It happens in every work environment, and salons are no exception—particularly in an industry in which the workforce is more than 80% female (although men are also victims of harassment).

Sexual harassment can take two forms. The Equal Employment Opportunity Commission (EEOC) breaks it down into two categories: *quid pro quo* and *hostile environment.* The former means harassment that involves threats or rewards. For example, a harasser may threaten to fire you, or not give you a raise, or promise a raise in return for inappropriate behavior. A hostile environment is one in which you can't perform your job because of the intimidating or offensive working environment—for instance, if your boss or coworker is constantly making crude remarks, explicitly commenting on your appearance, or sending letters or calling you. It also includes assault and rape. The harasser needn't be a coworker or boss; he or she could also be a client, distributor, or someone else you have to deal with at work.

If you think you are a victim of sexual harassment, either confront the harasser and make your feelings known or otherwise demonstrate that you do not approve of the behavior. Sometimes perpetrators are unaware that what they are doing is making you uncomfortable. You need to tell them.

If the behavior continues, keep a record of what happens: What was said, who said it, when it was said, and whether there were witnesses. Keep any and all evidence. Ask your coworkers if they have experienced the same problems. If the harasser is a colleague or client, speak to your supervisor. If the harasser is your boss, contact the EEOC at 800-669-3362 or visit their website at www.eeoc.gov.

CONTINUING TO GROW

After a few years, there may come a time when you feel stale, even if you've managed to busy yourself with all the marketing ideas and extracurricular activities discussed in this chapter. You may feel particularly frustrated or bored if you haven't been promoted or don't see any more room for growth in your salon. When this happens, what should you do?

First, analyze why you feel the way you do. It may be that you really like your job but are overextended in other areas. Or you think you should be striving for more, to challenge your own comfort zone, even though you feel just fine and dandy where you are.

There may be more serious reasons as well. Maybe you're getting so much work doing photo shoots that the real-life clients in your chair don't present you with enough creative challenges. Or your haircolor skills have developed to the extent that you want to spearhead the development of a haircolor department within the salon, but the boss isn't keen on the idea.

Perhaps you're considering a job switch. Before you do anything, contemplate why you want to leave. If money is the primary reason, stop to consider that no matter how good you are you will lose up to about 50% of your clientele when you leave your current salon. Think how long it took you to build your current clientele. You worked hard, right? Well, you will have to work just as hard to rebuild it at the new salon. If a salon offers you a higher salary or commission but doesn't offer profit sharing, a savings plan, or a medical plan, you may wind up working harder for the same money you would have made if you stayed put.

If you're truly frustrated by what you're doing on a day-to-day basis in the salon, you have two options: Talk to your boss about how you feel and try to work out a solution, or find another position. Which option you choose is up to you. If you have a very sound and open relationship with your boss, you may feel comfortable discussing your unhappiness. But if you feel in your heart that you need a change of scenery as much as a change of job, then don't bring it up. For instance, if what you really want is to work as a hairstylist on movie sets, then there's nothing your boss can do for you other than wish you well.

Handling a Resignation

There are many reasons why people leave one job for another, but to maintain a good reputation within the beauty industry, it's important to act professionally when you actually quit a job. Getting into a fight with your boss, shouting, "I quit!" and then stomping out is never the best way to handle things. In the heat of anger, it is crucial to never let your negative feelings cause you to act unprofessionally. Don't view your resignation as an opportunity to get all of your negative feelings off your chest. While it might feel good for a moment, it will have a lasting effect on your career and on people's perception of you. Someone you told off could one day become manager of your new salon or might be able to help you down the line. The beauty industry is a close-knit community and in most areas, people in the business usually know one another, either in person or by reputation.

Similarly, if you get into a major disagreement with your employer, never make a decision to quit impulsively. Cool down for a few days and think about your decision. If you decide it's time to move on, start looking for a new job before actually resigning. As a general rule, even if you're not getting along with your boss or coworkers, it's never a good idea to quit your current job until you've lined up a new one.

While you are looking for a new job, keep your plans to yourself. Don't broadcast your unhappiness to clients. Talk about your interests and ambitions, if you like (client connections can give your career a tremendous boost), but be discreet so the whole salon doesn't have to hear about them.

Wait for the right job. Even if your boss is making you miserable or the rest of the staff just walked out, you don't need to jump into the first available lifeboat. If you do, you could find yourself even more miserable than before in three months' time. (The exception: If you sense that the salon is about to go out of business and you need to maintain a steady income.)

Remember how far you've come. It may take weeks, months, and even years to find your next ideal position, but you will find it. In the meantime, focus on your own professional agenda, and remember that not so long ago you didn't know how to do foil.

Once you've landed that new job, arrange a private meeting with the salon manager or with the appropriate person at the salon and offer your resignation in-person, following it up in writing with a friendly and professional letter. You should be prepared to give your current employer the customary two weeks notice. It is not acceptable to give notice and then use accumulated vacation or sick days to avoid showing up for work. Even if your new employer wants you to start work immediately, they should understand that as a matter of professional courtesy, it is necessary for you to stay with your current employer for two weeks after giving your notice.

During those last two weeks on the job, offer to do whatever you can to maintain positive relationships with the other stylists and manager. Purposely causing problems, complaining to clients about the salon, stealing, trying to turn other stylists to your way of thinking or otherwise sabotaging the business are all actions that are unethical and inappropriate. Some salons will request your immediate departure when you quit, in part to reduce the chance that you will take client information with you. This is especially true if you're leaving on a negative note. Prior to quitting, try to determine how past coworkers were treated, so you will know what to expect.

When you leave the salon for the last time, take with you only your personal belongings and nothing that is considered the salon's property. Make a point to return your keys and anything belonging to the salon that was in your possession. If possible, for your protection, obtain a written memo stating that everything was returned promptly and in working order.

Down the road, you might need to use your current employer as a reference. Simply walking off the job and leaving them in a bind is not the best way to maintain positive relationships.

With a little forethought and planning, your first year as a beauty professional will lead seamlessly into a thriving career. Remember to keep a clear view of your goals, both long-term and short-term, and you will be assured of meeting them. Most of all, keep a positive attitude and you will have a positive career.

THE INSIDE TRACK

Who:	Jackie Perez
What:	Esthetician
Where:	San Juan, Puerto Rico

I work in a major resort hotel and spa in San Juan. For three and a half years I have performed facials and aromatherapy treatments on the guests who visit the property. Often, while their husbands are golfing, the women congregate in the spa—for massages, facials, and manicures. Lately, the spa is being booked by more and more men. Not content to leave with a simple massage, they are indulging in facials more than ever—for that healthy vacation glow. At first, the men and women feel shy about their indulgences or about their perceived flaws. By the end of the 45-minute session, however, they are excited about their appearance and relaxed after being pampered by soothing scents and a gentle touch.

I started my professional training in San Juan right after high school. I've always felt passionate about beauty and style. As a teenager, I had to be the first girl to read the fashion magazines at our school library, and I did my best to copy the latest look. I loved MTV and E! and visited the make-up counters every Saturday afternoon at the mall to try out new and outrageous trends. All of my friends and sisters came to me for makeup and hair styling before school dances, and I enjoyed bringing out the best in all of them.

For the women in my family, beauty was always a priority. We were fortunate to have good genes when it comes to skin. My great grandmother didn't see her first wrinkle until she was in her eighties and my grandmother and mother are often mistaken for sisters. As I got older, I realized that I needed to take care of my skin in order to keep it looking young. I started asking questions of my older female relatives regarding their skincare regimens. Simple, natural cleansers, treatments, and moisturizers made from milk, oatmeal, rice, and fruits of the island were their beauty staples. I decided to blend my formal training with my family household remedies and came up with some excellent fresh products. Soon, I had a neighborhood following. At work, I used only the spa-sanctioned products, but in the past year, I began showing my supervisors some of my potions and techniques. For four months, I've been incorporating some special treatments into my standard facials—for breakouts, for dry skin, and for aging skin. The results have been wonderful. I'm booked every day in the spa, as word of mouth travels from guest to guest at the pool. Many of my happy customers tell me that they look forward to seeing me next year, and ask for products to take home to the Untied States. For now, I give them free samples, but who knows—maybe in a year I will have my own product line!

For me, having my own small line of skincare products is my ultimate goal. I love the smile of a customer who has realized her beauty once I have helped her uncover what was there all along, waiting to emerge from layers of damaged skin.

My advice for people interested in beauty is to go for it! Don't let anyone discourage you from this exciting career. Training and apprenticing can seem like a long time, but it's worth it in the end. You may feel like you're never going to make money, but stick with it—soon you will have a clientele and a comfortable salary. You will meet many interesting people and never have two work days the same. And, the opportunities for work are many and varied. I never thought I would be working at a top international hotel company, but here I am, just five years out of beauty school.

Professional Associations and State Cosmetology Boards

IN ADDITION to contact information for professional organizations, this appendix contains a state-by-state list of cosmetology associations.

PROFESSIONAL ASSOCIATIONS

Below is a list of organizations that you can contact for further information about different segments of the professional beauty industry. Also included is contact information for accrediting organizations and placement services.

Advanstar Communications' International Beauty Group
7500 Old Oak Boulevard
Cleveland, OH 44130
440-243-8100
Fax: 440-891-2727
e-mail: information@advanstar.com

This organization provides clients with an integrated marketing approach, from magazines to trade events, and other marketing tools. They offer over 120 years of experience in the beauty industry. They publish the renowned beauty magazines *American Spa* and *American Salon*, and put on the International Beauty Show (IBS) each year in New York City and Long Beach, CA. They also hold the yearly Haircolor USA tradeshow in Miami.

American Association of Cosmetology Schools (AACS)
15825 North 71st Street
Suite 100
Scottsdale, AZ 85254-1521
480-281-0431
Fax: 480-905-0708
e-mail: ditsah@beautyschools.org
www.beautyschools.org

AACS keeps member schools abreast of changes in federal and state laws and regulations. AACS offers its members educational services, promotes the welfare of cosmetology education, and establishes a unity of spirit and understanding among institutions and their instructional staff in their efforts to pursue the goals and resolve the problems related to postsecondary cosmetology education.

American Beauty Association (ABA)
P.O. Box 809199
Chicago, IL 60680-9199
312-245-1595
Fax: 312-245-1080
www.abbies.org

ABA serves as the lobbying, organizational, and networking association for the professional salon industry.

American Board of Certified Master Haircolorists
P.O. Box 9090
San Pedro, CA 90734
888-425-6578 or 310-547-0814
www.haircolorist.com

This relatively young organization offers haircolor education through a home-study course that prepares colorists to take a three-part certification examination, offered at sites throughout the United States.

American Hair Loss Council (AHLC)
30 Grassy Plain Road
Bethel, CT 06801
888-873-9719
e-mail: membership@ahlc.org
www.ahlc.org

AHLC is a nonprofit organization that provides the public with nonbiased information on treatments and options for men, women, and children experiencing hair loss. Members include cosmetologists, barbers, manufacturers, physicians, and other specialists.

Associated Bodywork & Massage Professionals (ABMP)
1271 Sugarbush Drive
Evergreen, CO 80439-9766
303-674-8478 or 800-458-2267
Fax: 303-674-0859
e-mail: expectmore@abmp.com
www.abmp.com

ABMP promotes ethical practices and legitimate standards of training, protects the rights of practitioners, and educates the public about the benefits of massage, bodywork, and somatic therapies. Membership benefits include professional liability insurance, regulatory interaction, and health insurance.

Beauty & Barber Supply Institute (BBSI)
15825 North 71st Street
Suite 100
Scottsdale, AZ 58254
800-468-BBSI or 480-281-0424
Fax: 480-905-0708
www.bbsi.org

BBSI is the national association of whole-salers, including distributors, manufacturers, and manufacturers' reps.

Cosmetologists Chicago (CCA)
401 N. Michigan Avenue
Chicago, IL 60611
312-321-6809 or 800-648-2505
Fax: 312-245-1080
e-mail: info@isnow.com
www.isnow.com

CCA produces the large Midwest Beauty Show, held every February or March at the Rosemont Convention Center in Rosemont, IL. CCA offers educational programs on hair, skin, body, cosmetics, and nails to both members and nonmembers.

Cosmetology Advancement Foundation (CAF)
PMB 102
4262 Northlake Boulevard
Palm Beach Gardens, FL 33410-0344
561-630-7766
Fax: 561-630-0344
www.cosmetology.org

CAF's mission is to develop a unified approach to issues and trends affecting the salon industry and to seek opportunities to improve the industry's image, growth, and development.

The Day Spa Association
P.O. Box 5232
West New York, NJ 07093
201-865-2065
Fax: 201-865-3961
e-mail: info@dayspaassociation.com
www.dayspaassociation.com

The Day Spa Association promotes member spas and spa-related businesses by listing them in a membership directory distributed to consumers and the spa industry all over the country and on the Web.

International Chain Salon Association (ICSA)
Route 61-N
P.O. Box 600
Pottsville, PA 17901
717-429-1800
Fax: 717-429-1143
www.icsa.cc

ICSA's members include approximately 50 chain salon organizations throughout North America and Europe. ICSA members own and operate more than 7,000 salons that employ more than 45,000 people. ICSA was established to help chain salons grow in size and strength.

International Nail Technicians Association
401 North Michigan Avenue
Chicago, IL 60611
312-321-5161
Fax: 312-245-1080
e-mail: trackman@sba.com
www.isnow.com

Nail Manufacturers Council (NMC)
401 N. Michigan Avenue
Chicago, IL 60611
312-245-1595
Fax: 312-245-1080
www.abbies.org/nmc.html

A division of the American Beauty Association, NMC represents the interests of manufacturers and manufacturers' reps.

National Accrediting Commission of Cosmetology Arts and Sciences (NACCAS)
901 Stuart Street, Suite 900
Arlington, VA 22203
703-527-7600
www.naccas.org

This institution establishes standards and accredits cosmetology schools, making them eligible to participate in federal loan programs.

National Alliance of Salon Professionals (NASP)
P.O. Box 4307
Tallahassee, FL 32315
888-385-3330
Fax: 850-526-4988
e-mail: nasp@naspgold.com

NASP promotes education and career advancement through 24-hour resources, a bimonthly newsletter, professional networking, legislative representation, certification, and educational programs.

National Association of Barber Boards (NABB)
77 S. High Street, 16th Floor
Columbus, OH 43266-0304
614-466-5003
Fax: 614-644-8112

Founded in 1935, this organization promotes the exchange of information among state barber boards and state agencies that examine, license, and regulate the barber industry; and aims to improve standards and procedures for examining barbers and regulating the barber industry.

National Cosmetology Association (NCA)
401 N. Michigan Avenue
Chicago, IL 60611
312-527-6757
Fax: 312-464-6110
e-mail: Gordon_Miller@sba.com
www.salonprofessionals.org

NCA, which was founded in 1921, represents more than 30,000 licensed cosmetologists and salon owners across the country. NCA's interests and activities include every sector of the industry—hairdressers, estheticians, nail technicians, salon owners, school owners, and cosmetology students.

National-Interstate Council of State Boards of Cosmetology Inc. (NIC)
P.O. Box 11390
Columbia, SC 29211
718-519-6861
Fax: 718-519-7679
e-mail: jinnywilson@nictesting.org

NIC is a non-profit organization comprised of state board members from all 50 states as well as the District of Columbia, Guam, and Puerto Rico. NIC promotes an exchange of ideas, professionalism, and standardization of regulations, and it offers national examinations for license of cosmetology and related fields.

Professional Beauty Federation
2550 M Street, NW
Washington, DC 20037
703-527-7600 ext.33
Fax: 703-527-8811
e-mail: mkgross@erols.com
www.probeautyfederation.org

The Professional Beauty Federation is a non-profit corporation "dedicated to promote and protect the professional beauty industry as it relates to government laws and regulation." They are made up of licensed professionals, professional salons, currently enrolled cosmetology students, cosmetology schools, distributors, and manufacturers.

The Salon Association (TSA)
15825 North 71st Street
Suite 100
Scottsdale, AZ 85254
480-281-0429
Fax: 480-905-0708
www.salons.org

TSA's mission is to help salon owners find and share business solutions. It offers business education and creates member benefits and services that enhance salons' business environment.

Vocational Industrial Clubs of America (VICA)
P.O. Box 3000
Leesburg, VA 20177-0300
703-737-0607
Fax: 703-777-8999
e-mail: twh@skillsusa.org
www.skillsusa.org

VICA is a nonprofit organization that develops programs in tandem with vocational and technical schools.

STATE BOARDS OF COSMETOLOGY

Getting in touch with your state board can provide you with a wealth of benefits, including a lobbying voice in your state legislature, networking contacts, and important information on new laws. They will also provide you with information about joining your state's cosmetology association (if it has one).

Alabama
Alabama Board of Cosmetology
RSA Union Building
100 N. Union Street, #320
Montgomery, AL 36130
334-242-1918
Fax: 334-242-1926
e-mail: cosmetology@aboc.state.al.us
www.aboc.state.al.us

Alaska
Division of Occupational Licensing
Board of Barber & Hairdressers
P.O. Box 110806
Juneau, AK 99811-0806
907-465-2547
Fax: 907-465-2974
e-mail: cindy_evans@dced.state.ak.us
www.dced.state.ak.us/occ/pbah.htm

Arizona
State Board of Cosmetology
1721 F. Broadway Road
Tempe, AZ 85282-1611
480-784-4539
Fax: 480-255-3680
www.revenue.state.az.us/609/
     licensingguide.htm

Arkansas
Arkansas Board of Cosmetology
101 East Capitol, Suite 108
Little Rock, AR 72201
501-682-2168
Fax: 501-682-5640
e-mail: cosmo@mail.state.ar.us
www.accessarkansas.org/cos

California
Board of Barbering and Cosmetology
P.O. Box 944226
Sacramento, CA 94244-2260
916-327-6250
Fax: 916-445-8893
www.dca.ca.gov/barber

Colorado
State of Colorado Board of Barbers and
    Cosmetologists
1560 Broadway, Suite 1340
Denver, CO 80202
303-894-7772
www.dora.state.co.us/Barbers_
    Cosmetologists

Connecticut
Department of Public Health
Division of Health Systems Regulation
410 Capitol Avenue, MS #12APP
P.O. Box 34308
Hartford, CT 06134-0308
860-509-7569
www.state.ct.us/dph/Licensure/licensure.htm

Delaware
State of Delaware Board of Cosmetology
    and Barbering
P.O. Box 1401
Dover, DE 19903
302-736-4796
Fax: 302-739-2711
www.state.de.us/license/24/index.htm

Florida
Department of Business and Professional
    Regulation
1940 North Monroe Street
Tallahassee, FL 32399
850-488-5702
Fax: 850-922-6959

Georgia
Secretary of State/Examining Boards
    Division
166 Pryor Street SW
Atlanta, GA 30303-3465
404-657-3907
Fax: 404-651-9532
www.sos.state.ga.us/plb/barber_cosmet

Hawaii
State of Hawaii Professional and Vocational
    Licensing Division
Department of Commerce and Consumer
    Affairs
Board of Cosmetology
P.O. Box 3469
Honolulu, HI 96801
808-586-3000
Fax: 808-586-2699
www.state.hi.us/dcca/pvl/
    areas_barbering.html

Idaho
Idaho State Board of Cosmetology
Department of Self-Governing Agencies
Bureau of Occupational Licenses
1109 Main Street, Suite 220
Boise, ID 83705-2598
208-334-3233
www2.state.id.us/ibol/cos.htm

Illinois
Illinois Department of Professional
    Regulation
320 West Washington Street, 3rd Floor
Springfield, IL 62786
217-785-7729
Fax: 217-782-7645
www.dpr.state.il.us/WHO/cosmo.asp

Indiana
Indiana Professional Licensing Agency
302 West Washington Street, Suite E034
Indianapolis, IN 46204-2246
317-232-2980
Fax: 317-232-2312
www.in.gov/pla/bandc/cosmetology

Iowa
Board of Cosmetology Arts & Science
321 Lucas State Office Building
Des Moines, IA 50319
515-281-4422
Fax: 515-281-3121
e-mail: scook@idph.state.ia.us
www.idph.state.ia.us/idph_pl/licensure/
cosmetology_licensure_index.html

Kansas
Kansas State Board of Cosmetology
714 S.W. Jackson
Topeka, KS 66617
785-296-3155
Fax: 785-296-3002

Kentucky
State Board of Hairdressers and
Cosmetologists
111 St. James Court
Frankfort, KY 40601
502-564-4262
Fax: 502-564-0481

Louisiana
State Board of Cosmetology
11622 Sunbelt Court
Baton Rouge, LA 70809
225-756-3404
Fax: 225-756-3410

Maine
Department of Professional and Financial
Regulation
Licensing and Enforcement Division
35 State House Station
Augusta, ME 04333-0035
207-624-8603
Fax: 207-624-8637
www.state.me.us/pfr/olr

Maryland
State Board of Cosmetologists
500 North Calvert Street
Room 307
Baltimore, MD 21202-3651
410-230-6320
www.dllr.state.md.us/license/cosmet/cosmeti
ntro.html

Massachusetts
Commonwealth of Massachusetts
Division of Professional Licensure
Board of Registration of Cosmetologists
239 Causeway Street
Boston, MA 02114
617-727-3074
Fax: 617-727-2197
www.state.ma.us/reg/boards/hd/default.htm

Michigan
Bureau of Commercial Services
Board of Cosmetology
P.O. Box 30018
Lansing, MI 48909
517-241-9201
Fax: 517-241-9280
e-mail: bcsinfo@cis.state.mi.us
www.cis.state.mi.us/bcs/cos

Minnesota
Minnesota Department of Commerce,
    Cosmetology Unit
133 East Seventh Street
St. Paul, MN 55101
651-296-6319 or 800-657-3978
Fax: 612-296-2886
www.commerce.state.mn.us/pages/
    CosmetologyMain.htm

Mississippi
Mississippi State Board of Cosmetology
1808-1808 North State Street
P.O. Box 55689
Jackson, MS 39296-5689
601-354-6623
Fax: 601-354-7176

Missouri
Missouri State Board of Cosmetology
3605 Missouri Boulevard P.O. Box 1062
Jefferson City, MO 65102
573-751-2000
Fax: 573-751-8167
www.ecodev.state.mo.us/pr/cosmo

Montana
Montana State Board of Cosmetology
301 South Park
P.O. Box 200513
Helena, MT 59620-0513
406-841-2333
Fax: 406-444-1667
www.discoveringmontana.com/dli/bsd/
    license/bsd_boards/cos_board/board_
    page.htm

Nebraska
Nebraska Board of Cosmetology Examiners
Nebraska Department of Health and Human
    Services
Regulation and Licensure Credentialing
    Division
P.O. Box 94986
Lincoln, NE 68509-5007
402-471-2117
Fax: 402-471-3577
www.hhs.state.ne.us/crl/mhcs/cosindex.htm

Nevada
State Board of Cosmetology
1785 East Sahara Avenue, Suite 255
Las Vegas, NV 89104
702-486-6542
Fax: 702-369-8064
e-mail: nvcosmbd@govmail.state.nv.us
www.state.nv.us/cosmetology

New Hampshire
State Board of Barbering, Cosmetology and
    Esthetics
2 Industrial Park Drive
Concord, NH 03301
603-271-3608
Fax: 603-271-6702
http://webster.state.nh.us/cosmet

New Jersey
New Jersey State Board of Cosmetology and
    Hairstyling
124 Halsey Street, 6th Floor
Newark, NJ 07101
973-504-6400
www.state.nj.us/lps/ca/nonmed.htm

New Mexico
New Mexico Board of Barbers and
    Cosmetologists
Regulation and Licensing Department
P.O. Box 25101
Santa Fe, NM 87504
505-827-7550
Fax: 505-827-7560
www.rld.state.nm.us/b&c/barber_and_
    cosmetologist_board.htm

New York
New York Department of State
Division of Licensing Services
84 Holland Avenue
Albany, NY 12208-3490
518-473-2731
Fax: 518-473-6648
e-mail: info@dos.state.ny.us
www.dos.state.ny.us/lcns/cosmain.html

North Carolina
State Board of Cosmetic Art
1201 Front Street #110
Raleigh, NC 27609
919-733-4117
Fax: 919-733-4127
www.cosmetology.state.nc.us

North Dakota
North Dakota State Board of Cosmetology
P.O. Box 2177
Bismarck, ND 58502
701-223-9800
Fax: 701-222-8756

Ohio
State Board of Cosmetology
101 Southland Mall
Columbus, OH 43207-4041
614-466-3834
Fax: 614-644-6880
e-mail: ohiocosbd@cos.state.oh.us.
www.state.oh.us/cos

Oklahoma
State Board of Cosmetology
2200 Classen Boulevard
Suite 1530
Oklahoma City, OK 73107
Phone: 405-521-2441
Fax: 405-528-8310
www.oklaosf.state.ok.us/~cosmo

Oregon
Oregon Health Division Licensing Programs
700 Summer Street NE, Suite 100
Salem, OR 97301
503-378-2114 (information, ext. 4300;
    licensing, ext. 4307; exam, ext. 4304)
Fax: 503-370-9004
e-mail: hlo.info@state.or.us
www.hdlp.hr.state.or.us/bhhome.htm

Pennsylvania
Bureau of Professional and Occupational
    Affairs
Department of State
State Board of Cosmetology
P.O. Box 2649
Harrisburg, PA 17105-2649
717-783-7130
Fax: 717-705-5540
e-mail: cosmetol@pados.dos.state.pa.us
www.dos.state.pa.us/bpoa/cosbd/mainpage.
    htm

Rhode Island
Department of Health
Division of Hairdressing and Barbering
Three Capitol Hill
Providence, RI 02908-5097
401-277-2511 or 401-277-2827
Fax: 401-222-1272
www.health.state.ri.us/hsr/hair_barb.htm

Appendix A

South Carolina
P.O. Box 11329
Columbia, SC 29211
803-896-4494
Fax: 803-896-4484
www.llr.state.sc.us/POL/Cosmetology/
Default.htm

South Dakota
Department of Commerce and Regulation
Cosmetology Commission
500 East Capitol
Pierre, SD 57501-5070
605-773-6193
Fax: 605-224-5072
www.state.sd.us/dcr/cosmo/cosmo-ho.htm

Tennessee
State Board of Cosmetology
Davy Crockett Tower 1st Floor
500 James Robertson Parkway
Nashville, TN 37243-1147
615-741-2515 or 800-480-9285
Fax: 615-741-1310
e-mail: egriffin@mail.state.tn.us
www.state.tn.us/commerce/cosmo

Texas
Texas Cosmetology Commission
5717 Balcones Drive
P.O. Box 26700
Austin, TX 78755-0700
512-454-4674
Fax: 512-454-0399
www.txcc.state.tx.us

Utah
Utah State Board of Cosmetology/Barbers
Division of Occupation and Professional
Licensing
160 East, 300 South
P.O. Box 45805
Salt Lake City, UT 84145-0805
801-530-6536
Fax: 801-530-6511
www.commerce.utah.gov/DOPL/dopl1.htm

Vermont
Vermont Board of Cosmetology
109 State Street
Montpelier, VT 05609-1101
802-828-2837
Fax: 802-828-2384
www.vtprofessionals.org/cosmetologists

Virginia
Commonwealth of Virginia, Department of
Commerce
Department of Professional Occupation and
Regulation
Board of Cosmetology
2600 West Broad Street
Richmond, VA 23230-4917
804-367-8509
Fax: 804-367-2475
www.state.va.us/dpor/cos_main.htm

Washington
Department of Licensing
Professional Licensing Services,
Cosmetology Section
P.O. Box 9026
Olympia, WA 98504
360-753-3834
Fax: 360-664-2550
www.wa.gov/dol/bpd/cosfront.htm

West Virginia
State Board of Barbers and Cosmetologists
1716 Pennsylvania Avenue, Suite 7
Charleston, WV 25302
304-558-2924
Fax: 304-558-3450
www.wvdhhr.org/pages/bca/barbers.htm

Wisconsin
Department of Regulation of Licensing
Barbering and Cosmetology Examining
    Board
P.O. Box 8935
Madison, WI 53708-8935
608-266-5511 or 608-266-2112
Fax: 608-267-3816
www.state.wi.us/agencies/drl

Wyoming
Wyoming Board of Cosmetology
26th & House Avenue, Suite 302
Cheyenne, WY 82002
307-777-3534
Fax: 307-777-5700
soswy.state.wy.us/director/ag-bd/cosmet.htm

Additional Resources

THIS APPENDIX contains a list of books, magazines, and web-sites that can assist you in your job search and your professional development.

FINDING THE RIGHT COLLEGE & PAYING FOR IT

Books

Best 331 Colleges: 2001 Edition (Princeton, NJ: Princeton Review, 2001).

Cassidy, Daniel J. *The Scholarship Book 2001: The Complete Guide to Private-Sector Scholarships, Fellowships, Grants, and Loans for the Undergraduate* (Englewood Cliffs, NJ: Prentice Hall Press, 2001).

The College Board College Cost & Financial Aid Handbook 2001 (College Entrance Examination Board, 2000).

The College Board Index of Majors and Graduate Degrees 2001 (New York, College Entrance Examination Board, 2000).

Kaplan Guide to the Best Colleges in the U.S. 2001 (New York: Kaplan Publishing, 2000).

Occupational Outlook Handbook (U.S. Department of Labor, 2000).

Peterson's Guide to Two-Year Colleges 1998: The Only Guide to More than 1,500 Community and Junior Colleges. (Princeton, NJ: Peterson's, 1998).

Peterson's Guide to Colleges for Careers in Computing (Princeton, NJ: Peterson's Guides, 1996).

CAREER AND JOB HUNTING GUIDANCE

Books

Bolles, Richard Nelson. *What Color Is Your Parachute? 2000: A Practical Manual for Job Hunters and Career Changers* (Berkeley, CA: Ten Speed Press, 1999).

Graber, Steven. *The Everything Get-A-Job Book: From Resume Writing to Interviewing to Finding Tons of Job Openings* (Holbrook, MA: Adams Media Corporation, 2000).

Eyre, Vivian V., Jennifer Williams, and Diane Osen. *Great Interview: Successful Strategies for Getting Hired* (New York: LearningExpress, 2000).

Rich, Jason R. *Great Resume: Get Noticed, Get Hired* (New York: Learning-Express , 2000).

Rich, Jason R. *Job Hunting for the Utterly Confused* (New York: McGraw-Hill, 1998).

Rich, Jason R. *The Unofficial Guide to Earning What You Deserve* (Indianapolis, IN: Macmillan, 1999).

Rich, Jason R. *Your Career: Coach Yourself to Success* (New York, Learning-Express, 2001).

Rothman, Wendy Alfus and Kate Wendleton. *Targeting the Job You Want: Featuring Special Sections throughout on Using the Internet to Identify and Reach Your Job Targets* (Franklin Lakes, NJ: The Career Press, 2000).

Smith, Rebecca. *Electronic Resumes & Online Networking: How to Use the Internet to Do a Better Job Search, Including Complete, Up-to-date Resource Guide* (Franklin Lakes, NJ: The Career Press, 1999).

Online

The Web is an extremely powerful job search tool that can not only help you find exciting job opportunities, but also research companies, network with other people in your field, and obtain valuable career-related advice.

Using any internet search engine or portal, you can enter keywords such as: *resume, cosmetology jobs, cosmetology career, cosmetology job listings,* or *help wanted* to find thousands of websites of interest to you. The following is a listing of just some of the online resources available to you.

1st Impressions Career Site—www.1st-imp.com

1, 2, 3 Jobs.com—www.123-jobs.com

ABA Resume Writing—www.abastaff.com/career/resume/resume.htm

About.com—
http://jobsearch.about.com/jobs/jobsearch/msubrespost.htm

Accent Resume Writing—www.accent-resume-writing.com/critiques

Altavista Career Center—www.careers.altavista.com

Advanced Career Systems—
www.resumesystems.com/career/Default.htm

America's Employers—www.americasemployers.com

America's Job Bank—www.ajb.dni.us

America's Job Bank—www.ajb.dni.us

Best Jobs USA—www.bestjobsusa.com

Boldface jobs—www.boldfacejobs.com

Boston Herald's Job Find—www.jobfind.com

A Career.com—www.acareer.com

Career & Resume Management for the 21st Century—
http://crm21.com

Career Avenue—www.careeravenue.com

Career Builder—www.careerbuilder.com

Career Center—www.jobweb.org/catapult/guenov/res.html#explore

Career City—www.careercity.com

Career Creations—www.careercreations.com

Career Express—www.careerxpress.com

Career Magazine—www.careermag.com

Career Resumes—www.career-resumes.com

Career Shop—www.careershop.com

Career Spectrum—www.careerspectrum.com/dir-resume.htm

Career.com—www.career.com

CareerMosaic—www.careermosaic.com

CareerNet—www.careers.org

CareerPath—www.careerpath.com

CareerWeb—www.cweb.com

Confident Resume—www.tcresume.com

Creative Professional Resumes—www.resumesbycpr.com

Electronic Resume.com—www.electronic-resume.com

First Job: The Web Site—www.firstjob.com

First Resume Store International—www.resumestore.com

First Resume Writing Services—www.firstjobresumes.com

Freeagent.com—www.freeagent.com

Gary Will's Worksearch—www.garywill.com/worksearch

Get a New Job.com—www.getanewjob.com

Headhunter.net—www.headhunter.net

Hot Jobs.com—www.hotjobs.com

JobBank USA—www.jobbankusa.com

Job Hunting Tips—www.job-hunting-tips.com

Job Island—www.jobisland.com

JobLynx—www.joblynx.com

JobNet.org—www.jobnet.org

Jobs Online—www.jobsonline.com

Job Options—www.joboptions.com

Jobs.com—www.jobs.com

Job Search.com—www.jobsearch.com

JobSource—www.jobsource.com

JobStar—http://jobsmart.org/tools/resume

JobTrack—www.jobtrack.com

Kforce.com—www.kforce.com

Kaplan Online Career Center—www.kaplan.com

Medzilla.com—www.medzilla.com

Monster Board—www.monster.com

My Job Search.com—www.myjobsearch.com

Professional Association of Resume Writers—
    www.parw.com/homestart.html

Proven Resumes—www.provenresumes.com

Resume Net—www.resumenet.com

Resume Office—www.resumeoffice.com

Resume Station—www.resumestation.com

Quintessential Careers—www.quintcareers.com/resres.html

Rebecca Smith's eResumes & Resources—www.eresumes.com

Resumania—www.resumania.com

Resume—www.wm.edu/csrv/career/stualum/resmdir/contents.htm

Resume Broadcaster—www.resumebroadcaster.com

Resume Magic—www.liglobal.com/b_c/career/res.shtml

Resume Plus—www.resumepls.com

Resume.com—www.resume.com

Resumedotcom—www.resumedotcom.com

Salary.com—www.salary.com

Taos Careers—www.taos.com/resumetips.html

Ultimate Jobs—www.ultimatejobs.com

Vault.com—www.vaultreports.com/jobBoard/SearchJobs.cfm

Virtual Resume—www.virtualresume.com

A Write Impression—www.awriteimpression.com

Yahoo Careers—careers.yahoo.com

POPULAR INTERNET SEARCH ENGINES

To find additional online resources that can help you write your resume, find job opportunities in cosmetology, apply for jobs online, gather company or industry research, or network with people in cosmetology, visit any of the popular internet search engines and choose keywords or search phrases you think will help you find the specific information you're looking for.

Some of the popular search engines and information portals on the internet include:

All-In-One Search	www.allonesearch.com
AltaVista	www.altavista.com
AOL	www.aol.com
Ask Jeeves	www.askjeeves.com
Dogpile	www.dogpile.com
Excite	www.excite.com
Google	www.google.com
Hotbot	www.hotbot.com
Infoseek	www.infoseek.com
Lycos	www.lycos.com

MSN	search.msn.com
Savvy Search	www.savvysearch.com
Snap	www.snap.com
The Go Network	www.go.com
Web Crawler	www.webcrawler.com
Yahoo!	www.yahoo.com

COSMETOLOGY RESOURCES

Books

Cotter, Louise and Frances London Dubose. *The Transition: How to Become a Salon Professional* (Albany: Milady Publishing Corporation, 1996).

D'Angelo, Allen R. *Fun, Creative, & Profitable Salon Marketing: 67 Ways to Grow for Salon Business* (Winter Park, FL: Archer-Ellison Publishing, 1998).

Dunlap, Kathi A. *Adding It Up: Math for Your Cosmetology Career* (Albany: Delmar Publishing, 1992).

Gambino, Henry J. *The Esthetician's Guide to Business Management* (Albany: Milady Publishing Corporation, 1994).

Gearhart, Susan Wood. *Opportunities in Beauty Culture Careers* (Lincoln, IL: NTC Publishing Group, 1996).

Gerson, Joel. *Milady's Standard Textbook for Professional Estheticians* (Albany: Milady Publishing Corporation, 1998).

Heavilin, Shelley, ed. *Milady's Illustrated Cosmetology Dictionary* (Albany: Milady Publishing Corporation, 2001).

Larson, Mark and Barney Hoskyns. *The Mullet: Hairstyle of the Gods* (London: Bloomsbury Publishing, 2000).

Lytle, Elizabeth Stewart. *Careers in Cosmetology* (New York: The Rosen Publishing Group, 1999).

Maurer, Gretchen. *The Business of Bridal Beauty* (Albany: Milady Publishing Corporation, 1998).

Milady's Art and Science of Nail Technology, 1997 Edition (Albany: Milady Publishing Corporation, 1997).

Milady's Standard Textbook of Cosmetology, 2000 Edition (Albany: Milady Publishing Corporation, 1999).

Oppenheim, Robert. *101 Salon Promotions* (Albany: Milady Publishing Corporation, 1999).

McCormick, Janet. *Spa Manicuring for the Salon and Spa* (Albany: Milady Publishing Corporation, 1999).

Phillips, Carol. *In the Bag: Selling in the Salon* (Albany: Milady Publishing Corporation, 1994).

Spear, J. Elaine. *Salon Client Care: How to Maximize Your Potential for Success* (Albany: Milady Publishing Corporation, 1999).

Strazzabosco, Jeanne M. *Choosing a Career in Cosmetology* (New York: The Rosen Publishing Group, 1996).

Wiggins, Joanne L. and Ron Wiggins. *Milady's Guide to Owning and Operating a Nail Salon* (Albany: Milady Publishing Corportation, 1994).

Magazines

Trade magazines are a valuable source of information on trends, techniques, and business for the salon professional. Contact any or all of the following:

American Salon
270 Madison Avenue
New York, NY 10016
www.americansalonmag.com

American Spa
www.americanspamag.com

Cosmetic World
www.cosmeticworld.com

Dermascope
2611 N. Belt Line Road, Suite 140
Sunnyvale, TX 75182
972-226-2309
Fax: 972-226-2339
e-mail: dermascope@aol.com
www.dermascope.com

Modern Salon
847-634-2600
e-mail: driemer@vancepublishing.com
www.modernsalon.com

NailPro
www.nailpro.com

Nails Magazine
2021061 South Western Avenue
Torrance, CA 90501
310-533-2400
Fax: 310-533-2504
e-mail: nailsmag@nailsmag.com

Process
www.modernsalon.com

Salon News
5 East 34th Street
New York, NY 10001

Salon Today
www.modernsalon.com

Skin Inc.
362 South Schmale Road
Carol Stream, IL 60188-2787
800-469-7445 or 815-734-1147
www.skininc.com

Snip Magazine Inc.
1947 S. Wadsworth Boulevard #113
Lakewood, CO 80227
www.snipmagazine.com

Websites

directory.google.com/Top/Health/Beauty

A portal to many more beauty industry information websites and information about cosmetology schools.

www.abbies.org

The website of the American Beauty Association

www.beautytech.com

Here you'll find information on booth rental issues, live chat rooms, a message center, business support for salons, and a job posting site called Spa/Salon Staffing Services.

www.behindthechair.com

Industry information from information about trends, to training, to tips, in any aspect of the beauty industry.

www.clubspausa.com

Website for the Day Spa Association—for both consumers and professionals, it includes a national day spa directory and other industry information for day spa professionals.

www.dayspamag.com

An online magazine including training opportunities, classified ads, articles, and coming soon, an online beauty store.

www.fashion-beauty.com

This site is full of free fashion and beauty information for consumers and professionals. Visit this site for advice, industry news, and tips.

www.hairboutique.com

Follow industry trends and get up-to-date fashion news at this site.

www.hair-news.com

A website devoted to salon industry professionals—includes information, tips, continuing education, and more.

www.hairstylist.com

This site features style options for consumers and pros.

www.modernsalon.com

The official website of modern salon media, which includes modern salon, salon today and process magazines—for salon professionals, salon owners, and providers of professional salon services and products.

www.naccas.org

This site, for the National Accrediting Commission of Cosmetology Arts and Sciences, has a job bank and a resume bank for beauty professionals, as well as an annual report, legislative updates, a list of accredited schools, and application forms for financial aid.

www.oneroof.org

Portal site to industry information for salon and spa owners, cosmetology students and schools, and industry distributors, manufacturers, and sales representatives.

Portal to:

    Beauty and Barber Supply Institute—
        www.bbsi.org
    The Salon Association—www.salons.org
    The American Association of
        Cosmetology Schools—www.beau-
        tyschools.org

www.robertcraig.com

This site provides information on haircolor for consumers and professionals from haircolor whiz Robert Craig.

www.salonprofessionals.org

The official site of the National Cosmetology Association.

www.salonweb.com

This site offers chat rooms, product information, style tips, surveys, and job listings.

Appendix C

Sample Free Application for Federal Student Aid (FAFSA)

ON THE following pages you will find a sample FAFSA. Use this form to familiarize yourself with the form so that when you apply for federal, and state student grants, work-study, and loans you will know what information you need to have ready. When this book went to press, this was the most current form, and although the form remains mostly the same from year to year, you should check the FAFSA website (www.fafsa.ed.gov) for the most current information.

2001-2002

The FAFSA

July 1, 2001 — June 30, 2002
Free Application for Federal Student Aid

OMB # 1845-0001

Use this form to apply for federal and state* student grants, work-study, and loans.

Apply over the Internet with

FAFSA ON THE WEB **www.fafsa.ed.gov**

1 If you are filing a **2000 income tax return,** we recommend that you complete it before filling out this form. However, you do not need to file your income tax return with the IRS before you submit this form.

If you or your family has **unusual circumstances** (such as loss of employment) that might affect your need for student financial aid, submit this form, and then consult with the financial aid office at the college you plan to attend.

You may also use this form to apply for **aid from other sources, such as your state or college.** The deadlines for states (see table to right) or colleges may be as early as January 2001 and may differ. You may be required to complete additional forms. Check with your high school guidance counselor or a financial aid administrator at your college about state and college sources of student aid.

2 Your answers on this form will be read electronically. Therefore:

- use black ink and fill in ovals completely:
- print clearly in CAPITAL letters and skip a box between words:
- report dollar amounts (such as $12,356.41) like this:

Yes ● No ✕ ✍

| 1 | 5 | | E | L | M | | S | T |

$ | | 1 | 2 | , | 3 | 5 | 6 | **no cents**

Green is for students and purple is for parents.

If you have questions about this application, or for more information on eligibility requirements and the U.S. Department of Education's student aid programs, look on the Internet at **www.ed.gov/studentaid** You can also call 1-800-4FED-AID (1-800-433-3243) seven days a week from 8:00 a.m. through midnight (Eastern time). TTY users may call 1-800-730-8913.

3 After you complete this application, make a copy of it for your records. Then **send the original of pages 3 through 6** in the attached envelope or send it to: Federal Student Aid Programs, P.O. Box 4008, Mt. Vernon, IL 62864-8608.

You should submit your application as early as possible, but no earlier than January 1, 2001. We must receive your application **no later than July 1, 2002.** Your school must have your correct, complete information by your last day of enrollment in the 2001-2002 school year.

You should hear from us within four weeks. If you do not, please call 1-800-433-3243 or check on-line at www.fafsa.ed.gov

4 **Now go to page 3 and begin filling out this form. Refer to the notes as needed.**

STATE AID DEADLINES

AR	April 1, 2001 *(date received)*
AZ	June 30, 2002 *(date received)*
*^ CA	March 2, 2001 *(date postmarked)*
* DC	June 24, 2001 *(date received by state)*
DE	April 15, 2001 *(date received)*
FL	May 15, 2001 *(date processed)*
HI	March 1, 2001
^ IA	July 1, 2001 *(date received)*
IL	First-time applicants – September 30, 2001
	Continuing applicants – July 15, 2001
	(date received)
^ IN	For priority consideration – March 1, 2001
	(date postmarked)
* KS	For priority consideration – April 1, 2001
	(date received)
KY	For priority consideration – March 15, 2001
	(date received)
^ LA	For priority consideration – April 15, 2001
	Final deadline – July 1, 2001
	(date received)
^ MA	For priority consideration – May 1, 2001
	(date received)
MD	March 1, 2001 *(date postmarked)*
ME	May 1, 2001 *(date received)*
MI	High school seniors – February 21, 2001
	College students – March 21, 2001
	(date received)
MN	June 30, 2002 *(date received)*
MO	April 1, 2001 *(date received)*
MT	For priority consideration – March 1, 2001
	(date postmarked)
NC	March 15, 2001 *(date received)*
ND	April 15, 2001 *(date processed)*
NH	May 1, 2001 *(date received)*
^ NJ	June 1, 2001 if you received a
	Tuition Aid Grant in 2000-2001
	All other applicants
	– October 1, 2001, for fall and spring terms
	– March 1, 2002, for spring term only
	(date received)
*^ NY	May 1, 2002 *(date postmarked)*
OH	October 1, 2001 *(date received)*
OK	For priority consideration – April 30, 2001
	Final deadline – June 30, 2001
	(date received)
OR	May 1, 2002 *(date received)*
* PA	All 2000-2001 State Grant recipients and all
	non-2000-2001 State Grant recipients in
	degree programs – May 1, 2001
	All other applicants – August 1, 2001
	(date received)
PR	May 2, 2002 *(date application signed)*
RI	March 1, 2001 *(date received)*
SC	June 30, 2001 *(date received)*
TN	May 1, 2001 *(date processed)*
*^ WV	March 1, 2001 *(date received)*

Check with your financial aid administrator for these states: AK, AL, *AS, *CT, CO, *FM, GA, *GU, ID, *MH, *MP, MS, *NE, *NM, *NV, *PW, *SD, *TX, UT, *VA, *VI, *VT, WA, WI, and *WY.

^ *Applicants encouraged to obtain proof of mailing.*

* *Additional form may be required*

STATE AID DEADLINES

Notes for questions 13–14 (page 3)

If you are an eligible noncitizen, write in your eight or nine digit Alien Registration Number. Generally, you are an eligible noncitizen if you are: (1) a U.S. permanent resident and you have an Alien Registration Receipt Card (I-551); (2) a conditional permanent resident (I-551C); or (3) an other eligible noncitizen with an Arrival-Departure Record (I-94) from the U.S. Immigration and Naturalization Service showing any one of the following designations: "Refugee," "Asylum Granted," "Indefinite Parole," "Humanitarian Parole," or "Cuban-Haitian Entrant." If you are in the U.S. on only an F1 or F2 student visa, or only a J1 or J2 exchange visitor visa, or a G series visa (pertaining to international organizations), you must fill in oval **c**. If you are neither a citizen nor eligible noncitizen, you are not eligible for federal student aid. However, you may be eligible for state or college aid.

Notes for questions 17–21 (page 3)

For undergraduates, full time generally means taking at least 12 credit hours in a term or 24 clock hours per week. 3/4 time generally means taking at least 9 credit hours in a term or 18 clock hours per week. Half time generally means taking at least 6 credit hours in a term or 12 clock hours per week. Provide this information about the college you plan to attend.

Notes for question 29 (page 3) — Enter the correct number in the box in question 29.

Enter **1** for 1st bachelor's degree
Enter **2** for 2nd bachelor's degree
Enter **3** for associate degree (occupational or technical program)
Enter **4** for associate degree (general education or transfer program)
Enter **5** for certificate or diploma for completing an occupational, technical, or educational program of less than two years
Enter **6** for certificate or diploma for completing an occupational, technical, or educational program of at least two years
Enter **7** for teaching credential program (nondegree program)
Enter **8** for graduate or professional degree
Enter **9** for other/undecided

Notes for question 30 (page 3) — Enter the correct number in the box in question 30.

Enter **0** for 1st year undergraduate/never attended college
Enter **1** for 1st year undergraduate/attended college before
Enter **2** for 2nd year undergraduate/sophomore
Enter **3** for 3rd year undergraduate/junior
Enter **4** for 4th year undergraduate/senior
Enter **5** for 5th year/other undergraduate
Enter **6** for 1st year graduate/professional
Enter **7** for continuing graduate/professional or beyond

Notes for questions 37 c. and d. (page 4) and 71 c. and d. (page 5)

If you filed or will file a foreign tax return, or a tax return with Puerto Rico, Guam, American Samoa, the Virgin Islands, the Marshall Islands, the Federated States of Micronesia, or Palau, use the information from that return to fill out this form. If you filed a foreign return, convert all figures to U.S. dollars, using the exchange rate that is in effect today.

Notes for questions 38 (page 4) and 72 (page 5)

In general, a person is eligible to file a 1040A or 1040EZ if he or she makes less than $50,000, does not itemize deductions, does not receive income from his or her own business or farm, and does not receive alimony. A person is not eligible if he or she itemizes deductions, receives self-employment income or alimony, or is required to file Schedule D for capital gains.

Notes for questions 41 (page 4) and 75 (page 5) — only for people who filed a 1040EZ or Telefile

On the 1040EZ, if a person answered "Yes" on line 5, use EZ worksheet line F to determine the number of exemptions ($2,800 equals one exemption). If a person answered "No" on line 5, enter 01 if he or she is single, or 02 if he or she is married.

On the Telefile, use line J to determine the number of exemptions ($2,800 equals one exemption).

Notes for questions 47–48 (page 4) and 81–82 (page 5)

Net worth means current value minus debt. If net worth is one million or more, enter $999,999. If net worth is negative, enter 0.

Investments include real estate (do not include the home you live in), trust funds, money market funds, mutual funds, certificates of deposit, stocks, stock options, bonds, other securities, education IRAs, installment and land sale contracts (including mortgages held), commodities, etc. Investment value includes the market value of these investments as of today. Investment debt means only those debts that are related to the investments.

Investments do not include the home you live in, cash, savings, checking accounts, the value of life insurance and retirement plans (pension funds, annuities, noneducation IRAs, Keogh plans, etc.), or the value of prepaid tuition plans.

Business and/or investment farm value includes the market value of land, buildings, machinery, equipment, inventory, etc. Business and/or investment farm debt means only those debts for which the business or investment farm was used as collateral.

Notes for question 58 (page 4)

Answer **"No"** (you are not a veteran) if you (1) have never engaged in active duty in the U.S. Armed Forces, (2) are currently an ROTC student or a cadet or midshipman at a service academy, or (3) are a National Guard or Reserves enlistee activated only for training. Also answer "No" if you are currently serving in the U.S. Armed Forces and will continue to serve through June 30, 2002.

Answer **"Yes"** (you are a veteran) if you (1) have engaged in active duty in the U.S. Armed Forces (Army, Navy, Air Force, Marines, or Coast Guard) or as a member of the National Guard or Reserves who was called to active duty for purposes other than training, or were a cadet or midshipman at one of the service academies, **and** (2) were released under a condition other than dishonorable. Also answer "Yes" if you are not a veteran now but will be one by June 30, 2002.

The 2001-2002 FAFSA

Free Application for Federal Student Aid
For July 1, 2001 — June 30, 2002

OMB # 1845-0001

Step One: For questions 1-34, leave blank any questions that do not apply to you (the student).

1-3. Your full name (as it appears on your Social Security Card)

1. LAST NAME	2. FIRST NAME	3. MIDDLE INITIAL
FOR INFORMATION ONLY	DO NOT SUBMIT	

4-7. Your permanent mailing address

4. NUMBER AND STREET (INCLUDE APT. NUMBER)

5. CITY (AND COUNTRY IF NOT U.S.)   6. STATE   7. ZIP CODE

8. Your Social Security Number   XXX – XX – XXXX

9. Your date of birth   / / 19

10. Your permanent telephone number   ( ) –

11-12. Your driver's license number and state (if any)

11. LICENSE NUMBER   12. STATE

13. Are you a U.S. citizen? Pick one. **See Page 2.**
- a. Yes, I am a U.S. citizen. .... ○ 1
- b. No, but I am an eligible noncitizen. **Fill in question 14.** ...... ○ 2
- c. No, I am not a citizen or eligible noncitizen. .... ○ 3

14. ALIEN REGISTRATION NUMBER   A

15. What is your marital status as of today?
- I am single, divorced, or widowed. ○ 1
- I am married/remarried. ○ 2
- I am separated. ○ 3

16. Month and year you were married, separated, divorced, or widowed   MONTH / YEAR

For each question (17 - 21), please mark whether you will be full time, 3/4 time, half time, less than half time, or not attending. **See page 2.**

		Full time/Not sure	3/4 time	Half time	Less than half time	Not attending
17.	Summer 2001	○ 1	○ 2	○ 3	○ 4	○ 5
18.	Fall 2001	○ 1	○ 2	○ 3	○ 4	○ 5
19.	Winter 2001-2002	○ 1	○ 2	○ 3	○ 4	○ 5
20.	Spring 2002	○ 1	○ 2	○ 3	○ 4	○ 5
21.	Summer 2002	○ 1	○ 2	○ 3	○ 4	○ 5

22. Highest school your father completed   Middle school/Jr. High ○ 1   High school ○ 2   College or beyond ○ 3   Other/unknown ○ 4

23. Highest school your mother completed   Middle school/Jr. High ○ 1   High school ○ 2   College or beyond ○ 3   Other/unknown ○ 4

24. What is your state of legal residence?   STATE

25. Did you become a legal resident of this state before January 1, 1996?   Yes ○ 1   No ○ 2

26. If the answer to question 25 is **"No,"** give month and year you became a legal resident.   MONTH / YEAR

27. Are you male? (Most male students must register with Selective Service to get federal aid.)   Yes ○ 1   No ○ 2

28. If you are male (age 18-25) and not registered, do you want Selective Service to register you?   Yes ○ 1   No ○ 2

29. What degree or certificate will you be working on during 2001-2002? **See page 2** and enter the correct number in the box.

30. What will be your grade level when you begin the 2001-2002 school year? **See page 2** and enter the correct number in the box.

31. Will you have a high school diploma or GED before you enroll?   Yes ○ 1   No ○ 2

32. Will you have your first bachelor's degree before July 1, 2001?   Yes ○ 1   No ○ 2

33. In addition to grants, are you interested in student loans (which you must pay back)?   Yes ○ 1   No ○ 2

34. In addition to grants, are you interested in "work-study" (which you earn through work)?   Yes ○ 1   No ○ 2

35. Do not leave this question blank. Have you ever been convicted of possessing or selling illegal drugs? If you have, answer "Yes," complete and submit this application, and we will send you a worksheet in the mail for you to determine if your conviction affects your eligibility for aid.   No ○ 1   Yes ○ 3

DO NOT LEAVE QUESTION 35 BLANK

For Help — (800) 433-3243

Step Two:
For questions 36-49, report your (the student's) income and assets. If you are married, report your spouse's income and assets, even if you were not married in 2000. Ignore references to "spouse" if you are currently single, separated, divorced, or widowed.

36. For 2000, have you (the student) completed your IRS income tax return or another tax return listed in **question 37**?

   a. I have already completed my return. ○ 1   **b.** I will file, but I have not yet ○ 2   **c.** I'm not going to file. **(Skip to question 42.)** ○ 3
                                                       completed my return.

37. What income tax return did you file or will you file for 2000?

   a. IRS 1040 .... ○ 1   **d.** A tax return for Puerto Rico, Guam, American Samoa, the Virgin Islands, the
   b. IRS 1040A, 1040EZ, 1040Telefile ...... ○ 2   Marshall Islands, the Federated States of Micronesia, or Palau. **See Page 2.** ...... ○ 4
   c. A foreign tax return. **See Page 2.** ...... ○ 3

38. If you have filed or will file a 1040, were you eligible to file a 1040A or 1040EZ? **See page 2.** Yes ○ 1 No ○ 2 Don't Know ○ 3

For questions 39-51, if the answer is zero or the question does not apply to you, enter 0.

39. What was your (and spouse's) adjusted gross income for 2000? Adjusted gross income is on IRS Form 1040–line 33; 1040A–line 19; 1040EZ–line 4; or Telefile–line I. $ ☐☐☐ , ☐☐☐

40. Enter the total amount of your (and spouse's) income tax for 2000. Income tax amount is on IRS Form 1040–line 51; 1040A–line 33; 1040EZ–line 10; or Telefile–line K. $ ☐☐ , ☐☐☐

41. Enter your (and spouse's) exemptions for 2000. Exemptions are on IRS Form 1040–line 6d or on Form 1040A–line 6d. For Form 1040EZ or Telefile, **see page 2.**   ☐☐

42-43. How much did you (and spouse) earn from working in 2000? Answer this question whether or not you filed a tax return. This information may be on your W-2 forms, or on IRS Form 1040–lines 7 + 12 + 18; 1040A–line 7; or 1040EZ–line 1. Telefilers should use their W-2's.   **You (42)** $ ☐☐☐ , ☐☐☐

   Your Spouse (43) $ ☐☐☐ , ☐☐☐

Student (and Spouse) Worksheets (44-46)

44-46. Go to Page 8 and complete the columns on the left of Worksheets A, B, and C. Enter the student (and spouse) totals in questions 44, 45, and 46, respectively. Even though you may have few of the Worksheet items, check each line carefully.

   Worksheet A (44) $ ☐☐☐ , ☐☐☐

   Worksheet B (45) $ ☐☐☐ , ☐☐☐

   Worksheet C (46) $ ☐☐☐ , ☐☐☐

47. As of today, what is the net worth of your (and spouse's) current **investments**? **See page 2.** $ ☐☐☐ , ☐☐☐

48. As of today, what is the net worth of your (and spouse's) current **businesses and/or investment farms**? **See page 2.** Do not include a farm that you live on and operate. $ ☐☐☐ , ☐☐☐

49. As of today, what is your (and spouse's) total current balance of cash, savings, and checking accounts? $ ☐☐☐ , ☐☐☐

50-51. If you receive veterans education benefits, for **how many months** from July 1, 2001 through June 30, 2002 will you receive these benefits, and **what amount** will you receive per month? Do not include your spouse's veterans education benefits.   **Months (50)** ☐☐

   Amount (51) $ ☐☐☐

Step Three:
Answer all seven questions in this step.

52. Were you born before January 1, 1978? .... Yes ○ 1 No ○ 2

53. Will you be working on a master's or doctorate program (such as an MA, MBA, MD, JD, or Ph.D., etc.) during the school year 2001-2002? .... Yes ○ 1 No ○ 2

54. As of today, are you married? (Answer "Yes" if you are separated but not divorced.) .... Yes ○ 1 No ○ 2

55. Do you have children who receive more than half of their support from you? .... Yes ○ 1 No ○ 2

56. Do you have dependents (other than your children or spouse) who live with you and who receive more than half of their support from you, now and through June 30, 2002? .... Yes ○ 1 No ○ 2

57. Are you an orphan or ward of the court or were you a ward of the court until age 18? .... Yes ○ 1 No ○ 2

58. Are you a veteran of the U.S. Armed Forces? **See page 2.** .... Yes ○ 1 No ○ 2

If you (the student) answer "No" to every question in Step Three, go to Step Four.
If you answer "Yes" to any question in Step Three, skip Step Four and go to Step Five.

(If you are a graduate health profession student, your school may require you to complete Step Four even if you answered "Yes" in Step Three.)

Step Four: Complete this step if you (the student) answered "No" to all questions in Step Three.

59. Go to page 7 to determine who is considered a parent for this step. What is your parents' marital status as of today?
(Pick one.)   Married/Remarried ○ 1   Single ○ 2   Divorced/Separated ○ 3   Widowed ○ 4

60-63. What are your parents' Social Security Numbers and last names?
If your parent does not have a Social Security Number, enter 000-00-0000

| 60. FATHER'S/STEPFATHER'S SOCIAL SECURITY NUMBER | X X X – X X – X X X X | 61. FATHER'S/ STEPFATHER'S LAST NAME | FOR INFORMATION ONLY |
| 62. MOTHER'S/STEPMOTHER'S SOCIAL SECURITY NUMBER | X X X – X X – X X X X | 63. MOTHER'S/ STEPMOTHER'S LAST NAME | DO NOT SUBMIT |

64. Go to page 7 to determine how many people are in your parents' household.

65. Go to page 7 to determine how many in question 64 **(exclude your parents)** will be college students between July 1, 2001 and June 30, 2002.

66. What is your parents' state of legal residence?   STATE

67. Did your parents become legal residents of the state in question 66 before January 1, 1996?   Yes ○ 1   No ○ 2

68. If the answer to question 67 is "No," give the month and year legal residency began for the parent who has lived in the state the longest.   MONTH / YEAR

69. What is the age of your older parent?

70. For 2000, have your parents completed their IRS income tax return or another tax return listed in **question 71**?
- **a.** My parents have already completed their return. ○ 1
- **b.** My parents will file, but they have not yet completed their return. ○ 2
- **c.** My parents are not going to file. **(Skip to question 76.)** ○ 3

71. What income tax return did your parents file or will they file for 2000?
- **a.** IRS 1040 .... ○ 1
- **b.** IRS 1040A, 1040EZ, 1040Telefile ..... ○ 2
- **c.** A foreign tax return. **See Page 2.** ...... ○ 3
- **d.** A tax return for Puerto Rico, Guam, American Samoa, the Virgin Islands, the Marshall Islands, the Federated States of Micronesia, or Palau. **See Page 2.** .... ○ 4

72. If your parents have filed or will file a 1040, were they eligible to file a 1040A or 1040EZ? **See page 2.**   Yes ○ 1   No ○ 2   Don't Know ○ 3

For questions 73 - 83, if the answer is zero or the question does not apply, enter 0.

73. What was your parents' adjusted gross income for 2000? Adjusted gross income is on IRS Form 1040–line 33; 1040A–line 19; 1040EZ–line 4; or Telefile–line I. $ ___ , ___

74. Enter the total amount of your parents' income tax for 2000. Income tax amount is on IRS Form 1040–line 51; 1040A–line 33; 1040EZ–line 10; or Telefile–line K. $ ___ , ___

75. Enter your parents' exemptions for 2000. Exemptions are on IRS Form 1040–line 6d or on Form 1040A–line 6d. For Form 1040EZ or Telefile, **see page 2.**   ___

76-77. How much did your parents earn from working in 2000? Answer this question whether or not your parents filed a tax return. This information may be on their W-2 forms, or on IRS Form 1040–lines 7 + 12 + 18; 1040A–line 7; or 1040EZ–line 1. Telefilers should use their W-2's.

Father/Stepfather (76) $ ___ , ___
Mother/Stepmother (77) $ ___ , ___

Parent Worksheets (78-80)

78-80. Go to Page 8 and complete the columns on the right of Worksheets A, B, and C. Enter the parent totals in questions 78, 79, and 80, respectively. Even though your parents may have few of the Worksheet items, check each line carefully.

Worksheet A (78) $ ___ , ___
Worksheet B (79) $ ___ , ___
Worksheet C (80) $ ___ , ___

81. As of today, what is the net worth of your parents' current **investments**? **See page 2.** $ ___ , ___

82. As of today, what is the net worth of your parents' current **businesses and/or investment farms**? **See page 2.** Do not include a farm that your parents live on and operate. $ ___ , ___

83. As of today, what is your parents' total current balance of cash, savings, and checking accounts? $ ___ , ___

Now go to Step Six.

Step Five: Complete this step only if you (the student) answered "Yes" to any question in Step Three.

84. **Go to page 7** to determine how many people are in your (and your spouse's) household.

85. **Go to page 7** to determine how many in question 84 will be college students between July 1, 2001 and June 30, 2002.

Step Six: Please tell us which schools should receive your information.

For each school (up to six), please provide the federal school code and your housing plans. Look for the federal school codes on the Internet at **www.fafsa.ed.gov**, at your college financial aid office, at your public library, or by asking your high school guidance counselor. If you cannot get the federal school code, write in the complete name, address, city, and state of the college.

86. 1ST FEDERAL SCHOOL CODE **OR** NAME OF COLLEGE / ADDRESS AND CITY — STATE — HOUSING PLANS
87. on campus ○ 1 / off campus ○ 2 / with parent ○ 3

88. 2ND FEDERAL SCHOOL CODE **OR** NAME OF COLLEGE / ADDRESS AND CITY — STATE
89. on campus ○ 1 / off campus ○ 2 / with parent ○ 3

90. 3RD FEDERAL SCHOOL CODE **OR** NAME OF COLLEGE / ADDRESS AND CITY — STATE
91. on campus ○ 1 / off campus ○ 2 / with parent ○ 3

92. 4TH FEDERAL SCHOOL CODE **OR** NAME OF COLLEGE / ADDRESS AND CITY — STATE
93. on campus ○ 1 / off campus ○ 2 / with parent ○ 3

94. 5TH FEDERAL SCHOOL CODE **OR** NAME OF COLLEGE / ADDRESS AND CITY — STATE
95. on campus ○ 1 / off campus ○ 2 / with parent ○ 3

96. 6TH FEDERAL SCHOOL CODE **OR** NAME OF COLLEGE / ADDRESS AND CITY — STATE
97. on campus ○ 1 / off campus ○ 2 / with parent ○ 3

Step Seven: Please read, sign, and date.

By signing this application, you agree, if asked, to provide information that will verify the accuracy of your completed form. This information may include your U.S. or state income tax forms. Also, you certify that you (1) will use federal and/or state student financial aid only to pay the cost of attending an institution of higher education, (2) are not in default on a federal student loan or have made satisfactory arrangements to repay it, (3) do not owe money back on a federal student grant or have made satisfactory arrangements to repay it, (4) will notify your school if you default on a federal student loan, and (5) understand that **the Secretary of Education has the authority to verify information reported on this application with the Internal Revenue Service.** If you purposely give false or misleading information, you may be fined $10,000, sent to prison, or both.

98. Date this form was completed.

MONTH / DAY / 2001 ○ or 2002 ○

99. Student signature (Sign in box)

1 **FOR INFORMATION ONLY.**

Parent signature (one parent whose information is provided in Step Four) (Sign in box)

2 **DO NOT SUBMIT.**

If this form was filled out by someone other than you, your spouse, or your parent(s), that person must complete this part.

Preparer's name, firm, and address

100. Preparer's Social Security Number (or 101)

101. Employer ID number (or 100)

102. Preparer's signature and date

1

SCHOOL USE ONLY:

D/O ○ 1

FAA SIGNATURE

1

Federal School Code

MDE USE ONLY:
Special Handle

Page 6   For Help — www.ed.gov/prog_info/SFA/FAFSA

Notes for questions 59–83 (page 5) Step Four: Who is considered a parent in this step?

Read these notes to determine who is considered a parent for purposes of this form. **Answer all questions in Step Four about them**, even if you do not live with them.

If your parents are both living and married to each other, answer the questions about them.

If your parent is widowed or single, answer the questions about that parent. If your widowed parent has remarried as of today, answer the questions about that parent **and** the person whom your parent married (your stepparent).

If your parents have divorced or separated, answer the questions about the parent you lived with more during the past 12 months. (If you did not live with one parent more than the other, give answers about the parent who provided more financial support during the last 12 months, or during the most recent year that you actually received support from a parent.) If this parent has remarried as of today, answer the questions on the rest of this form about that parent **and** the person whom your parent married (your stepparent).

Notes for question 64 (page 5)

Include in your parents' household (see notes, above, for who is considered a parent):
- your parents and yourself, even if you don't live with your parents, and
- your parents' other children if (a) your parents will provide more than half of their support from July 1, 2001 through June 30, 2002 or (b) the children could answer "No" to every question in Step Three, and
- other people if they now live with your parents, your parents provide more than half of their support, and your parents will continue to provide more than half of their support from July 1, 2001 through June 30, 2002.

Notes for questions 65 (page 5) and 85 (page 6)

Always count yourself as a college student. **Do not include your parents.** Include others only if they will attend at least half time in 2001-2002 a program that leads to a college degree or certificate.

Notes for question 84 (page 6)

Include in your (and your spouse's) household:
- yourself (and your spouse, if you have one), and
- your children, if you will provide more than half of their support from July 1, 2001 through June 30, 2002, and
- other people if they now live with you, and you provide more than half of their support, and you will continue to provide more than half of their support from July 1, 2001 through June 30, 2002.

Information on the Privacy Act and use of your Social Security Number

We use the information that you provide on this form to determine if you are eligible to receive federal student financial aid and the amount that you are eligible to receive. Section 483 of the Higher Education Act of 1965, as amended, gives us the authority to ask you and your parents these questions, and to collect the Social Security Numbers of you and your parents.

State and institutional student financial aid programs may also use the information that you provide on this form to determine if you are eligible to receive state and institutional aid and the need that you have for such aid. Therefore, we will disclose the information that you provide on this form to each institution you list in questions 86–97, state agencies in your state of legal residence, and the state agencies of the states in which the colleges that you list in questions 86–97 are located.

If you are applying solely for federal aid, you must answer all of the following questions that apply to you: 1–9, 13–15, 24, 27–28, 31–32, 35, 36–40, 42–49, 52–66, 69–74, 76-85, and 98–99. If you do not answer these questions, you will not receive federal aid.

Without your consent, we may disclose information that you provide to entities under a published "routine use." Under such a routine use, we may disclose information to third parties that we have authorized to assist us in administering the above programs; to other federal agencies under computer matching programs, such as those with the Internal Revenue Service, Social Security Administration, Selective Service System, Immigration and Natural-ization Service, and Veterans Administration; to your parents or spouse; and to members of Congress if you ask them to help you with student aid questions.

If the federal government, the U.S. Department of Education, or an employee of the U.S. Department of Education is involved in litigation, we may send information to the Department of Justice, or a court or adjudicative body, if the disclosure is related to financial aid and certain conditions are met. In addition, we may send your information to a foreign, federal, state, or local enforcement agency if the information that you submitted indicates a violation or potential violation of law, for which that agency has jurisdiction for investigation or prosecution. Finally, we may send information regarding a claim that is determined to be valid and overdue to a consumer reporting agency. This information includes identifiers from the record; the amount, status, and history of the claim; and the program under which the claim arose.

State Certification

By submitting this application, you are giving your state financial aid agency permission to verify any statement on this form and to obtain income tax information for all persons required to report income on this form.

The Paperwork Reduction Act of 1995

The Paperwork Reduction Act of 1995 says that no one is required to respond to a collection of information unless it displays a valid OMB control number, which for this form is 1845-0001. The time required to complete this form is estimated to be one hour, including time to review instructions, search data resources, gather the data needed, and complete and review the information collection. If you have comments about this estimate or suggestions for improving this form, please write to: U.S. Department of Education, Washington DC 20202-4651.

We may request additional information from you to ensure efficient application processing operations. We will collect this additional information only as needed and on a voluntary basis.

Worksheets

Do not mail these worksheets in with your application.
Keep these worksheets; your school may ask to see them.

Worksheet A
Calendar Year 2000

For question 44 Student/Spouse		For question 78 Parent(s)
$	Earned income credit from IRS Form 1040–line 60a; 1040A–line 38a; 1040EZ–line 8a; or Telefile–line L	$
$	Additional child tax credit from IRS Form 1040–line 62 or 1040A–line 39	$
$	Welfare benefits, including Temporary Assistance for Needy Families (TANF). Don't include food stamps.	$
$	Social Security benefits received that were not taxed (such as SSI)	$
$ **Enter in question 44.**		**Enter in question 78.** $

Worksheet B
Calendar Year 2000

For question 45 Student/Spouse		For question 79 Parent(s)
$	Payments to tax-deferred pension and savings plans (paid directly or withheld from earnings), including amounts reported on the W-2 Form in Box 13, codes D, E, F, G, H, and S	$
$	IRA deductions and payments to self-employed SEP, SIMPLE, and Keogh and other qualified plans from IRS Form 1040–total of lines 23 + 29 or 1040A–line 16	$
$	Child support **received** for all children. Don't include foster care or adoption payments.	$
$	Tax exempt interest income from IRS Form 1040–line 8b or 1040A–line 8b	$
$	Foreign income exclusion from IRS Form 2555–line 43 or 2555EZ–line 18	$
$	Untaxed portions of pensions from IRS Form 1040–lines (15a minus 15b) + (16a minus 16b) or 1040A–lines (11a minus 11b) + (12a minus 12b) excluding rollovers	$
$	Credit for federal tax on special fuels from IRS Form 4136–line 9 – nonfarmers only	$
$	Housing, food, and other living allowances paid to members of the military, clergy, and others (including cash payments and cash value of benefits)	$
$	Veterans noneducation benefits such as Disability, Death Pension, or Dependency & Indemnity Compensation (DIC) and/or VA Educational Work-Study allowances	$
$	Any other untaxed income or benefits not reported elsewhere on Worksheets A and B, such as worker's compensation, untaxed portions of railroad retirement benefits, Black Lung Benefits, Refugee Assistance, etc. **Don't include** student aid, Workforce Investment Act educational benefits, or benefits from flexible spending arrangements, e.g., cafeteria plans.	$
$	Cash **received**, or any money paid on your behalf, not reported elsewhere on this form	XXXXXXXX
$ **Enter in question 45.**		**Enter in question 79.** $

Worksheet C
Calendar Year 2000

For question 46 Student/Spouse		For question 80 Parent(s)
$	Education credits (Hope and Lifetime Learning tax credits) from IRS Form 1040-line 46 or 1040A-line 29	$
$	Child support **paid** because of divorce or separation. Do not include support for children in your (or your parents') household, as reported in question 84 (or question 64 for your parents).	$
$	Taxable earnings from Federal Work-Study or other need-based work programs	$
$	Student grant, scholarship, and fellowship aid, including AmeriCorps awards, that was reported to the IRS in your (or your parents') adjusted gross income	$
$ **Enter in question 46.**		**Enter in question 80.** $